GW01339037

High Street

Market Place

Bedford Street

THE BOOK OF WOBURN

FRONT COVER: The Market Square facing south about 1830 when the present Town Hall was built. The buildings that once stood where the green and war memorial are today may be seen on the SW and SE sides of the crossroads. This print appeared in a book in 1831 and the 'new' Town Hall can be seen in the centre. (JDP)

The old church after the alterations of 1830, from the east. On the left is the old parsonage; on the right is the school with the fire engine house in front of it. (JDP)

THE BOOK OF WOBURN

BY

KENNETH G. SPAVINS

Completed by his daughter
ANNE APPLIN

BARON
BUCKINGHAM
MM

Originally published in 1983
Second edition 2000

PUBLISHED BY BARON BOOKS OF BUCKINGHAM
IN THIS SECOND EDITION 2000
AND PRODUCED BY REDWOOD BOOKS LIMITED

© Anne Applin 2000

ISBN 0 86023 664 1

All rights reserved. No part of this publication may be reproduced, stored in a retrieval system, or transmitted, in any form or by any means, electronic, mechanical, photocopying, recording or otherwise, without the prior permission of Baron Books.

Any copy of this book issued by the Publishers as clothbound or as paperback is sold subject to the condition that it shall not by way of trade or otherwise, be lent, re-sold, hired out or otherwise circulated without the Publisher's prior consent, in any form of binding or cover other than that in which it is published, and without a similar condition including this condition being imposed on a subsequent publisher.

Contents

ACKNOWLEDGEMENTS	8
PREFACES BY CANON J. RALPH DEPPEN & REV PAUL RICHARD MILLER	9
FOREWORD BY THE MARQUESS OF TAVISTOCK	10
INTRODUCTION BY KENNETH G. SPAVINS	10
VALEDICTUM BY ANNE APPLIN	11
MANOR AND ABBEY	14
MANY MANSIONS	29
PRIVATE MEANS AND PUBLIC WORKS	46
THE NEW CHURCH	71
DISSENTERS	98
WOBURN WHEELS	102
THE SOCIAL SCENE	108
YESTERDAY AND TODAY	123
INTO THE MILLENNIUM	158
APPENDIX 1 INCUMBENTS OF WOBURN	169
2 EARLS AND DUKES OF BEDFORD	170
BIBLIOGRAPHY	171
INDEX	173

Acknowledgements

I should like to thank everyone who has contributed in any way to the writing and completion of this book. Many are acknowledged in the key to the captions and the Bibliography, but some are not. Among these latter are those who have held the subscription lists which were essential for the book to be launched at all. My father was particularly grateful to the Marquess of Tavistock for his interest and support and for the way in which he was allowed to use material from the Bedford archives and the Abbey; to Miss Patricia Bell, county archivist, Mr Christopher Pickford, assistant archivist and the Bedfordshire County Council photographer, Mr K. Whitbread; to Mrs Leigh-Lancaster for the use of her father, Harry Morrison's notes and those of Fred West. My father was especially indebted to Mr John Walker for his patient hours of photographic work on the illustrations, which have brought *The Book of Woburn* visually alive. To them all I add my own special 'thankyou' for their continued encouragement when I took on the task of completing the manuscript, and for the time they gave in helping me to trace the sources of information and illustrations — in some cases leading to the finding of more material. One such example concerns the endpapers. These are sections from a limited edition drawn by John Rowland, who was Chief Forester for the Abbey 1955-68. Mr Rowland lived for a time in Paris House in the Park and gave me some interesting information about some of its previous occupants. I know that my father obtained verbal permission to use all the material lent to him and I have endeavoured to confirm the different authorisations in writing. If, however, because of the circumstances in which the book has been completed, there is anyone who has not received due acknowledgement, the omission is quite unintentional and their contribution is, and has been, sincerely appreciated.

Last, but by no means least, I must mention the forbearance of my family over the past year in allowing me the time to bring the project to completion and encouraging me in the task, and also the support and guidance of my publisher, Clive Birch for, without his efforts, faith and expertise the manuscript would not have seen the light of day.

Prefaces

by Canon J. Ralph Deppen, Priest-in-Charge, Woburn Parish

Labours of love are far and few to find, at best. In days like these when everyone is or manages to be busy in the myriad pursuits that conspire for one's precious 'free time', efforts like those represented in this book are rare indeed. Indeed, passing strangers, as I am, and descendants of the passing generations of Woburn, are in debt to the author for his kindness in adding to knowledge and appreciation of their rich inheritance.

This book is the fruit of more than academic interest and antiquarian curiosity. It grows from a life heavily invested in the fabric and the activity of the author's parish church. This book is a kind of manual of devotion for him and a guide for pilgrims along the way.

by Paul Richard Miller, Vicar of Woburn

Over the past twenty-five years Woburn, and more particularly, Woburn Abbey, have become household names.

Countless thousands of visitors from all parts of Britain, and indeed from all over the world, have travelled to this central point of England to savour the delights of a premier stately home, rolling parkland, wild animal reserve and a village.

Yes, some may stop to record on film the architectural delights of Woburn village, but few could appreciate the wealth of history which lies behind the Woburn of today.

This book will provide a rich reward for those prepared to pause and ponder. It is the fruit of painstaking research and gives to resident and visitor alike a new and deeper perspective.

I write this at a time of much uncertainty in world affairs, in our national life and indeed in that of our own village. While all communities change — for that is the nature of living beings — Woburn will change more in the next twenty years than it has in the past eighty of this century. This book will give us insights into the past which will enable us to meet the challenge of the changes of the future. Perhaps, in a hundred years' time, a reader of this book will be inspired to follow Dodd and Parry and Spavins to research the past and give new signposts to future generations.

Foreword

by the Marquess of Tavistock

I am very grateful to Mr Kenneth Spavins for having undertaken such a detailed and fascinating study of Woburn and its churches. It is indeed of great interest because of the detail he has uncovered, not only about the churches but also the lifestyle and its inhabitants for many centuries.

This is the first work of its kind to have been written this century and is a truly intriguing record; one which I hope will prove as fascinating to others as it has to my family and me.

Tavistock

Introduction

by Kenneth G. Spavins

Much has been written about the Russells and Woburn Abbey, but for the last hundred years very little seems to have been written about Woburn itself. Many people, both local and visitors, have approached me concerning the history of both the old church and the present one. This book is intended to put on record at least some of the history of the place so that it may be passed on. I hope the reader will get as much enjoyment reading this book as I did with my research, and I should like to dedicate it to the Church of St Mary Woburn.

> Give instruction to a wise man,
> And he will be yet wiser:
> Teach just a man
> And he will increase in learning.
> The fear of the Lord
> Is the beginning of wisdom:
> And the knowledge of the Holy
> Is understanding.
>
> Proverbs

Valedictum

Kenneth Groom Spavins, my father, was a Bedfordshire man. Although he was born in Northamptonshire, at the age of three months he went to the village of Riseley in the north of Bedfordshire. There he spent his boyhood. When 14 he left school and began a lifetime's work 'on the land'. He experienced this century's agricultural revolution, which saw the transition from farming that depended upon horses and human muscle to a mechanised technology with its wholesale use of artificial fertilisers and pesticides. My father did not entirely approve of these changes and always retained a love for the countryside which recognised that it is better to work with Nature than against her.

As a boy, my father played the bugle in the Scout band, sang in the church choir and learnt to ring. His first peal was at Sharnbrook in 1947. He designed the badge of the Bedfordshire Association of Church Bell Ringers, was Secretary of its Luton District 1955-1975 and in 1976 was made a Vice-President of the Association. He was also elected a member of the Ancient Society of College Youths in 1957. Young ringers were taught by him on the clock bell of Woburn Old Church Tower (including myself and my mother), but it was often a struggle to maintain a full band for Sunday service ringing. A group of handbell ringers was a success for many years and they rang tunes as well as hymns and carols in the church. An annual event for several years was an invitation to play for the Duke and Duchess of Bedford in Woburn Abbey at Christmas. My mother now keeps the handbell tradition alive with the Girl Guides.

My father married Frances Parkinson in 1943 and she was a constant support to him. They continued to live at Riseley, where I was born, and then we moved to Woburn in 1955. It was here that my father became closely involved with the life of the church. He joined the choir almost as soon as we arrived (which was in the time of Rev T.N. Gunner) and shortly after took over from Douglas Harris as tower captain in charge of the bells. He was confirmed in the Parish Church and became churchwarden in 1967. Frequent enquiries by visitors about the history of the church led him to research and write a guide which, like Topsy, 'growed' to include the town's history.

Since his boyhood my father worked with wood. His first tools were bought for him by his foster mother and he used to do woodwork during the evenings in a small outhouse next to the tiny cottage in Riseley. He won the woodwork prize at school and gradually added to his collection of tools, which allowed him to turn his hand to a variety of projects. He made lamps that were sold in the Bedford shop of Hockliffe's, galleons (some of which went abroad with foreign troops as they returned home after the war), furniture which included reproduction antiques and clocks, scale-model carts and waggons, numerous carvings, love-spoons, bobbins and many large pieces for the Parish Churches in Riseley, Woburn and elsewhere. Indeed, his work for the Church added in reality to what Woburn is today. He turned his hand to other crafts, which included painting in oils and water colour and corn dolly making.

My father was most at home in the peace of the countryside, observing animals, listening to the birds and watching them nest in nest-boxes he made for them, and pottering in his workshop. His taste and sensitivity ranged from music to antiques, and his collection of old farm implements reflected his country roots and love of Nature. The enthusiasm with which he sought information for *The Book of Woburn* was also a reflection of his affection for the village and what it meant to him. By 1982, after about six years of research and enquiry, he had a basic text but, at the age of 65, having retired less than a year, he died suddenly and I took on the task of completing the manuscript and preparing it for publication.

I was 11 when we moved to Woburn and so my formative years were spent in the village until I went to University. I sang in the church choir and the Choral Society, which was conducted by Rev Gunner with Miss Lovell as its accompanist. Rev Gunner also taught me to play the organ and my father taught me to ring. I belonged to the Girl Guides for a time and then was Akela with the Cub Pack and secretary of the Youth Club in the time of Rev R.O. Osborne. Of all these clubs, sadly, only the Girl Guides remains. And so I have a knowledge and nostalgia of Woburn that enabled me to continue my father's work. Using his basic text and a few notes I began my own research. I tried to bring a related view to the Woburn seen through my father's eyes by means of an enquiring approach and wider vision. In this way the visual aspect of the book as well as the text was expanded, in an attempt to portray not only Woburn's origins and history but also Woburn now, as a record for the future. It has been a fascinating project but not without its difficult moments and I am grateful to everyone who has helped the work on its way. Indeed, in trying to confirm data and trace the owners of illustrations, yet more material has come to light. Some has been included but there is not room for it all — the story goes on.

The story of Woburn is one of a hamlet that grew and prospered with the increased trade that occurred when a monastery was founded nearby in the 12th century. In the 16th century the monastery passed from religious hands into those of the Russell family and Woburn's wealth and prosperity continued to increase during the coaching era. However, trading prosperity declined when the freight and passengers of the coaches were taken by the railways from stations elsewhere. Woburn town is once more a small village, its claim to fame still resting with the House of Bedford. It was my father's pleasure to begin writing the story of Woburn; it has been my pleasure to complete it on his outline. I hope that you who read it will share in that pleasure.

Anne Applin

September 1983

The author Kenneth G. Spavins in his workshop finishing the hymn board for the parish church in 1967. (BT)

ABOVE: The silver lavabo bowl made in 1979 by Garrard of London and bought for the church with the proceeds of a memorial fund for the author; (JW) BELOW: the set of Christmas figures given to the church by the author's family in his memory. They are hand carved in olive wood from the Holy Land. (JW)

Manor and Abbey

It would be exciting to speculate that a Roman track once passed through Woburn, over the crossroads that today form the main streets of the town. Indeed, with the Watling Street so near it might be thought highly likely. Viatores, in his book on Roman roads in the South East Midlands, does in fact suggest that a Roman road ran through the parish along the old road past Job's Farm, via Leighton Street and then through the Park along the drive running north-east from Star lodge. However, although this road is old there are apparently no positive signs of Roman construction. Over the centuries there has been little ground disturbance in the vicinity which might uncover a Roman settlement, although some Roman pottery vessels were apparently found at the Abbey a long time ago. It is therefore difficult to say if the town grew out of a Roman settlement. At present all the evidence points to the establishment of a community in Saxon times. Indeed, the derivation of the name *Woburn* is Saxon. Over the years it has been given a number of spellings such as Woubourne and Oobourne but, however spelt, the name derives from the Saxon *wo* meaning twisted or crooked, and *burn* meaning a stream. Certainly the Saxons and Angles would have found it useful to make a settlement near a stream, so that they could water their livestock, and it is thought that the stream which runs from Pinfold (an area on the outskirts of Woburn along the Leighton Buzzard road) to Husborne Crawley gave Woburn its name.

The earliest known record of Woburn is a 10th century document: in 969 King Edgar granted Aspley to his thegn Alfworld and that part of the boundary was

'up to the little knoll, thence to the apple tree where three land boundaries meet, of the men of Woburn, and of the men of Wavendon, and of the men of Aspley; from the deer-gate over the heath . . .'

Domesday Book of 1086 records that the manor of Woburn had been held by King Edward the Confessor's thegn Alric, at which time there were on it six sochmen (tenants who held land in return for ploughing their lord's land each year) who held two hides (200 acres) and 'could do with them what they pleased'. After the Conquest the manor was held by Walter Giffard, who rented it to Hugh de Bolebec. Approximately 2,400 acres were arable land, although only about 800 acres were actually cultivated at the time. The principal farm (demesne) covered 200 acres and eight villeins (more or less slaves who transferred with the land they worked from one owner to another) had 600 acres. There were seven bordars (tenants who had a house) and four servants. Meadowland covered 600 acres and there was enough woodland to support 100 hogs.

Not a great deal is known of Walter Giffard, but we do know more about Hugh de Bolebec, who eventually became seized of the manor in chief. He was of baronial descent and owned large estates in Buckinghamshire as well as in Bedfordshire.

In 1145, Hugh's grandson, also Hugh de Bolebec, founded the Abbey of St Mary at Woburn. He invited the Cistercian (reformed Benedictine) Order of monks at Fountains Abbey in Yorkshire to make a foundation on his land. The order had originated in France at Citeaux under Stephen Harding, an Englishman. The first Cistercian abbey in Bedfordshire was at Old Warden, founded in 1135 by Walter Espec from the early foundation at Rievaulx in Yorkshire and it may have been this example which inspired Hugh de Bolebec to make his invitation. J.D. Parry in his *History of Woburn Abbey* published in 1831 comments that:

'The situation jointly chosen by Hugh de Bolebec and the Abbot of Fountains for the new foundation, was a very appropriate and convenient one, occupying the exact site of the modern splendid edifice. It is sheltered on three sides by small hills and trees, and the front is notwithstanding sufficiently elevated to command a clear and open view, and with a prospect over the town of Woburn, then a small village. It also posses s facilities for the formation of fish-ponds on different levels, of which there are now three or four, and which was a very important object to the monks; as, from their constitutions prohibiting in general the eating of the flesh of quadrupeds, there was necessarily a considerable demand for such a supply: birds and fish, with a certain degree of license in eating flesh to the inland monasteries, constituting with fruits, and herbs, and corn, their entire sustenance.'

The Abbey itself was placed at a distance from both the hamlet of Woburn and the parish church of Birchmore close by, and the Abbot effectively became the lord of the manor. A manor was a consolidated estate run, at least in part, by labour service under its lord. Since the Cistercian Order was a secluded one, a local gentleman was appointed as a steward in the village to administer the estate and act between the abbot and the people, such as in the collection of rents.

Each year every Cistercian abbot had to visit Citeaux and all daughter houses of his abbey, so Woburn Abbey would have been visited regularly by the Abbot of Fountains. Indeed, in 1170, while Allan was still Abbot at Woburn, Abbot Richard of Fountains was returning from a general Chapter when he fell sick and died at Woburn Abbey. The name William occurs as Abbot of Woburn in about 1180 and it was in his abbacy that Henry II eventually granted a charter confirming the donations of Hugh de Bolebec and other subsequent benefactors.

We know that Peter was Abbot in 1202, for he was sent to Worcester to enquire into miracles which were alleged to have taken place there at the shrine of St Wulfstan. William was Abbot in 1204 and in 1217 Richard became Abbot. However, although an abbot may be an inspiring religious leader he is not necessarily good at management and, in 1234 when the abbey at Woburn was in debt, Abbot Richard was removed and Roger was sent from Fountains to replace him. For a time the monks were dispersed among neighbouring religious houses, St Albans Abbey and Dunstable Priory probably being their principal places of refuge. The Priory granted to Woburn 'our mill of Grenefeld in Flitwick, at perpetual farm, for 26s. the year' to help the Abbey become solvent again, other benefactors paid the debts and the Abbey was reopened 'with increased splendour'. The financial failure of Woburn may have been due, in part, to a food shortage caused by severe weather conditions. The monks did not spend all their time in contemplation — they worked hard to cultivate the land around them. When more land was acquired a grange would be built on it, consisting of a chapel and refectory with some lay brothers and a monk who stayed for a short time and then returned to the mother house. In this way abbeys became economic units. Woburn Abbey had two granges nearby. One was Utcote, (meaning Out Cottages) to the north-west of the Abbey; buildings called Utcoate Grange still stand along the Leighton Buzzard road just past Pinfold Pond. The other grange was Whitnoe, (meaning White spur of land) which was north of the Abbey. The house has disappeared and the site became kitchen gardens. Food supplies would have been limited and much affected by seasonal weather variations. Parry quotes an entry from an old *Annals* which shows there was a general scarcity of food at the time: 'An.Dom.1234. 18 Henry the 3. Was a great frost at Christmasse, which destroyed the corne in the ground, and the roots of hearbs in the gardens, continuing till candlemasse without any snow, so that no man could plough the ground, and all the yeare after was unseasonable weather, so that bareness of all things ensued, and many poor folkes dyed for want of victualls, the rich being so bewitched with avarice, that they could yield them no reliefe.'

The Abbey was not long in recovering and fifty years later was one of the wealthiest houses in the county. This was eventually to benefit the community at large for, in 1242, Henry III granted to the Abbot the right to hold a weekly market on Fridays 'at the chapel of old Woburn' and a yearly fair in September to last for three days. Thus, at the gates of the Abbey, Woburn was developing into a small market town.

Roger of Fountains was followed by Adam de Luton as Abbot of Woburn. Adam died in 1247, then Nicholas was elected; he was followed by Roger who died in 1281 and Hugh de Soulbury was elected. During his abbacy, Edward I, having returned from the Holy Land, ordered the Church to account for its administrations. And so in 1287 Abbot Hugh de Soulbury was called upon by the Crown to show by what right he claimed a view of frankpledge, market and fair in his manor of Woburn.

The *frankpledge* was a system by which all free men of a tithing were responsible for the general good behaviour of the members, and the 'view of frankplege' was a court which dealt with law-breakers. The Abbot appeared, and said that he held court twice a year, when the sheriff visited, and kept order among the people under his jurisdiction in the same way as the sheriff did in his court. However, he said that he held a charter of Hugh de Bolbec, confirmed by Henry II, which rendered him free from certain services generally laid on those holding land and that he had rule over men and property which were not subject to the King's control. He also referred to a charter which granted the holding of a weekly market and an annual three-day fair. This incident shows the general authority of the Abbey at the time . The Abbot won his case and it is fortunate that he did for, if the King had been granted the rights held by the monastery, the Abbey of St Mary at Woburn may well have been drained of its wealth and therefore unable to survive.

Details of daily life, services, studies etc in the monasteries are hard to come by for Bedfordshire in the 14th and 15th centuries and little is known of the Abbey at Woburn for the next two hundred years or so, information coming mainly from the chronicles of other monasteries. Woburn was then in the diocese of Lincoln but nothing is supplied by the Lincoln registers since, like all Cistercian houses, the Abbey was exempt from visitation. Some idea of the number of inmates in the late 14th century is given by tax returns. Warden Abbey was the largest with 24 monks and 6 lay brothers; the next were Woburn Abbey and Dunstable Priory each with 17 inmates. The Abbey must have flourished for J.D. Parry notes that in 1433 the 'Abbas de Woburn et Celerarii sui' were specified in a list of gentry, suggesting that there were two cellarers at Woburn, which was not general. One cellarer managed the indoor affairs and one the outdoor, implying that there was great business and importance attached to the Abbey. A cellarer was third in rank under the Abbot and 'was the Father of the whole society; he had the care of every thing relating to the food of the monks, and also of the vessels and household utensils of the whole society. He was to be careful of the healthy, but especially of the sick'.

He was, in effect, a house steward and was also in charge of the highways in the neighbourhood of the monastery, again showing the influence of Abbey on town.

Although little is known of the Abbey during these years, a great deal is known at the time of its dissolution under Henry VIII, because of the trial and execution of the last Abbot, Robert Hobbs. Depositions taken in 1538 show that there were at least 13 monks besides the Abbot, and probably a few lay brothers. There seems to have been no prior, and the most important person after the Abbot was the sub-prior. A 'bowser' or bursar had replaced the old cellarer, and other monks served as sexton, and 'chaunter' or precentor. One was secretary to the Abbot. Among outsiders, three 'young gentlemen' and their schoolmaster had recently been boarders in the Abbey and a former Abbot of Warden had retired there.

The 1530s brought to a head the uneasy relationship between Crown and Church. England was under the spiritual rule of the Pope, but Henry VIII wanted his marriage annulled and by 1532 had secured his independence from the Pope. Cranmer's court opened in Dunstable in 1533 to pronounce on the validity of Henry's marriage to Catherine of Aragon who was at the time residing at Ampthill, and in 1534-35 a visitation of monasteries was begun by the King's commissioners under Thomas Cromwell. The monks were required to take the oath of supremacy which stated that the King was head, on earth, of the Church in England and that the Pope's name was to be erased from all service books. The Abbot was known to have disliked the prospect of taking the oath of suprermacy and he expressed his uneasiness to many people. A few years earlier John Wylwarde, priest at Toddington, had sent Abbot Hobbs a book entitled *De potestate Petri* which set forth the argument for the Pope's supremacy. In return the Abbot had sent Wylwarde a book on a similar subject. The books had been taken to and fro by William Sherborne, a priest at the chapel in the town of Woburn. Few of the other monks shared the Abbot's views but nevertheless they were obedient to him to the last.

A preliminary visit was made to the abbey at Woburn by a Dr Petre who administered the oath of supremacy to the whole convent and ordered that all papal bulls were to be delivered to him and that the Pope's name was to be erased from all service books. However, Abbot Hobbs confessed afterwards that he had had the bulls copied before they were delivered to Dr Petre and had asked that the Pope's name be struck out with pen and not erased. During the next three years the new political and religious thinking was much discussed in the Abbey but only two monks were decidedly in favour of the new thinking and two or three were with the Abbot for the old way. The rest had no strong opinions at all. Meanwhile the Abbot became more conscience-stricken at his own cowardice in taking the oath of supremacy and, during a painful illness, said that he wished he had died with Sir Thomas More, Bishop Fisher and others who would not take the oath. His wish was soon to be granted for William Sherborne found some bulls which had not been given to Dr Petre and took them straight to London with a letter from Dan Robert Salford, one of the monks who shared his views. Sherborne had once been a friar, but was dismissed by the Pope and so was now in favour of the 'new thinking'. In May 1538 Dr Petre and his fellow commissioner John Williams arrived at the Abbey; goods were seized on 5 May and Williams took over the administration of the estate. On the 11th and 12th the monks were questioned by the commissioners, reports were taken to London by Williams, and as a result the Abbot, sub-prior and sexton were committed for trial.

The trial took place before nine commissioners at Abbot's Woburn on 14 June 1538, the Friday of Whitsun week. The Abbot offered no defence to the accusation that he had failed to preach the King's supremacy, and that he had openly expressed his opinions on the subject on many occasions. The sub-prior was accused of failing to preach the King's supremacy and of praying publicly for the Pope, and the sexton, Dan Laurence Blunham, was said to have openly boasted that he had never taken the oath and never would — he had been passed over in the crowd and had not kissed the book. The depositions of Dan Robert Salford, who had sent the letter to London, and of William Sherborne, who had taken it, also implicated others within and outside the monastery, but no action seems to have been taken. During the whole trial no charge was made against the personal character of any of the monks, and the monastery seems to have fallen for purely political reasons, since it was apparently in good order and the rule was well kept. Parry quotes information on Abbot Hobbs given to him by Jeremiah Wiffen, taken from manuscripts in the British Museum at that time (1831):

'He seems to have been a conscientious and pious man; fervent, it is true, in upholding the observances imposed by the Catholic church, but fulfilling his moral, conventual, and religious duties, in a manner that engaged the respect, not to say veneration, of his friends and his acquaintance. His society was courted by the nobility as well as clergy of his neighbourhood . . . From the crime and corruption which had tainted so great a number of the monastic establishments of the realm, his monastery was almost, if not entirely free.'

However, the jury had no alternative but to convict the three on the charges made against them and they were condemned to be executed. All three asked for the King's mercy but to no avail — verbal treason had been committed and could not be undone. The exact place of execution is not known. A strong local tradition says that they were hanged on an oak tree which is about 190 yards from the south-west corner of the west front of the present Abbey. Afterwards the Abbot was drawn and quartered. Loudoun, who apparently saw the tree in 1836, estimated its age to be 500 years then which means that in 1538 it was about 200 years old and today is nearly 650 years old! A recent boring showed that the tree is in fact hollow, but is maintaining itself, and could be about 500 years old. The exact date of execution is not known either. Though the trial was on 14 June, the first Ministers' Account showed the land as belonging to the Abbey until the 20th. Maybe this was the date of execution. Robert Hobbs sacrificed his life for his principles. This was unusual in Bedfordshire at that time; others were less principled or more cowardly; for example, Prior of Dunstable Gervase Markham, who complied with the King's demands, was given a sizeable pension of £60 a year.

Among Abbot Hobb's friends were not only clergy but also members of the nobility. They included Sir Francis Bryan who was a steward for the Abbey. Even before the trial the Abbot had given a ring to Thomas Lowe, asking him to give it to Sir Francis on his return to England, saying, 'I shall never see him again in this world, for especially I am compassed by craft of my mortal enemies, and they have set their time well, he being now out of the realm, and I have none so sure a friend as him to speak to the king's grace for me; I pray God he have good speed, and send him well home, and bid him to take care of compassers; and thus I pray thee heartily to recommend me unto him, beseeching him to pray for me, and to be good master unto my poor servants and friends.'

(Parry/Wiffen)

It is natural that the Abbot should have trusted as his steward a man who was already steward of the Royal estate at Ampthill, but Sir Francis Bryan does not appear to have been quite the person Abbot Hobbs supposed. On 16 July 1538 John Williams was appointed Receiver-General of the Woburn estate and almost immediately he and Bryan secured leases and divided the lands between them. Williams took Utcote grange with the land, meadows and the coney warren. Bryan had Whitnoe Grange with the site of the Abbey itself, the other coney warren and the great pond which lay, and lies today, between the town of Woburn and the Abbey. The bailiffs, Edward and Robert Staunton, accounted for the monastic lands at Woburn itself that Michaelmas and they record the rents paid by Bryan as £49 and that of Williams as £50. The two of them, therefore, seem to have divided Woburn between them as equally as they could.

In 1542 Woburn was added to the Royal estate (Honour) of Ampthill. Williams continued as Receiver-General and Bryan's activities centred round Ampthill rather than Woburn. In 1545 Bryan was called upon to prove that he had been steward for the Abbey at Woburn long before the dissolution. Since he had no document granted by the Abbot, he called upon two of the Abbey's former monks — William Stolt, late cellarer of the monastery and John Grace of Woburn, Clerk — and the Stauntons to confirm that he had received the grant of the stewardship from the Abbot, and that it was not cancelled by the forfeiture of the estate (attainder) at the dissolution in 1538. Bryan was particularly keen to prove this since he had arrears of fees owing to him from that date!

The leases to Williams and Bryan were renewed in 1545 and 1544 respectively, but Henry VIII died on 28 January 1547 and in his will granted land to the value of £100 a year to each of his executors. Among those named was John, Baron Russell of Chenies.

John Russell was a Dorset country gentleman and merchant. In 1506 Archduke Philip of Spain was driven ashore at Weymouth in a gale and John Russell's skill in languages made him of service to Henry VII. Russell accompanied the Archduke to court in London where he remained as a Gentleman Usher. He continued in loyal service to Henry VIII and Henry's children, and in Henry's will received not only Woburn but also land in Devonshire, Cornwall, Northamptonshire, Buckinghamshire and much of the property which once belonged to Thorney Abbey. Sir John was created 1st Earl of Bedford in 1550 by Edward VI but, for almost a hundred years, the family continued to live in their mansion at Chenies in Buckinghamshire, which John had acquired through a fortunate marriage; it is still the family's burial place.

The Abbey itself was not pulled down immediately nor lived in permanently until 1625, when Francis, who later became 4th Earl, sought refuge with his family from the plague in London, and decided to stay. The old Abbey was in poor condition and so the 4th Earl rebuilt it. Tradition says that a corridor in the present Abbey, called Paternoster Row, was built in 1626 where a corridor in the old monastery used to be. Only the North Wing of this 17th century building remains. By the 18th century the structure of the house was in need of repair and from 1750 it was gradually rebuilt. The house has been open to visitors by appointment since about 1780 and guide books were published from the early 19th century. It was opened to the general public by the present 13th Duke of Bedford in 1954 and is currently administered by the Marquess and Marchioness of Tavistock.

The seal of the abbey has not survived. The coat-of-arms of the Abbey was 'Azure three bars wavy argent'.

Abbots of Woburn

Alan, first abbot, 1145
William, occurs c1180
Peter, occurs 1202, died 1204
Nicholas, occurs 1208
Richard, occurs 1217, 1228, deposed 1234
Roger of Fountains, elected 1234
Adam of Luton, died 1247
Nicholas, elected 1247
Roger, died 1281
Hugh of Soulbury, elected 1281
William, occurs 1286
Henry, elected 1312
Robert de Stokes, elected 1297
Thomas de Thornton, elected 1336
John Upton
William Manepeny, elected 1396
William Hawburth, elected 1436
John of Ashby, elected 1458
Robert Charlet, elected 1463
Robert Hall, elected 1483
Thomas Hogeson, occurs 1499
Robert Hobbes, occurs 1529

LEFT: Pinfold stream, looking towards the present Utcoate Grange in January 1983; (A) RIGHT: looking north on the other side of the road; the stream is already wider; (A) BELOW: Pinfold Pond; (A) OPPOSITE: Pinfold Cottages; they once stood opposite Pinfold Pond but were demolished in the autumn of 1982. (CJR/SR)

ABOVE: Woburn's entry in the Domesday Book; (BCRO) BELOW: the old monastery/abbey of St Mary at Woburn, founded by Hugh de Bolebec in 1145; (JDP) OPPOSITE: a map showing the boundaries of the hundreds in the 11th century. (BCRO)

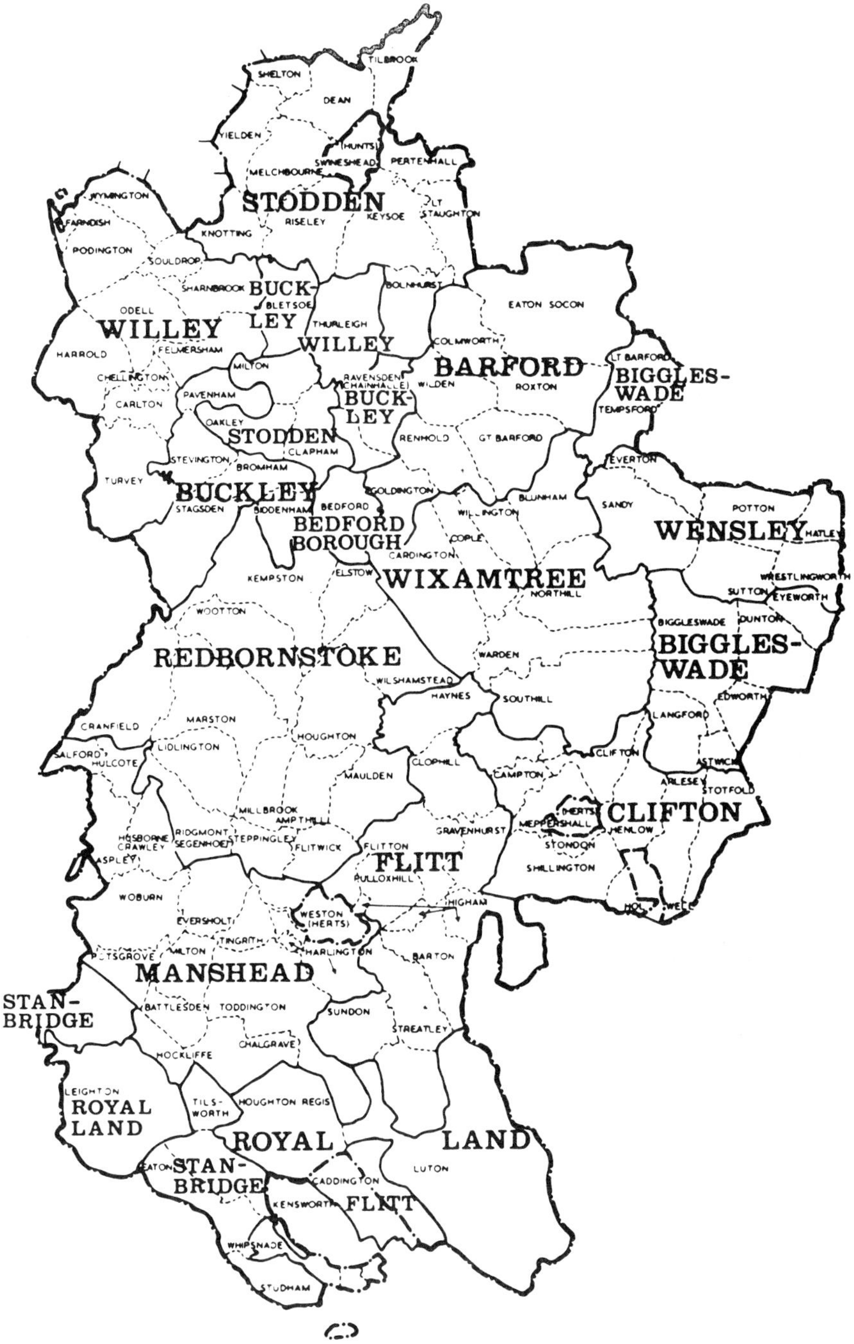
TILBROOK
SHELTON
DEAN
YIELDEN
(HUNTS)
SWINESHEAD
PERTENHALL
MELCHBOURNE
WYMINGTON
STODDEN
LT STAUGHTON
FARNDISH
KNOTTING
RISELEY
KEYSOE
PODINGTON
SOULDROP
SHARNBROOK
BUCK-LEY
BLETSOE
BOLNHURST
EATON SOCON
ODELL
WILLEY
THURLEIGH
HARROLD
FELMERSHAM
WILLEY
COLMWORTH
MILTON
BARFORD
LT BARFORD
BIGGLES-WADE
CHELLINGTON
RAVENSDEN
CHAINHALLE)
WILDEN
ROXTON
PAVENHAM
BUCK-LEY
TEMPSFORD
CARLTON
OAKLEY
STODDEN
RENHOLD
GT BARFORD
CLAPHAM
EVERTON
STEVINGTON
BROMHAM
TURVEY
GOLDINGTON
BLUNHAM
BUCKLEY
SANDY
POTTON
STAGSDEN
BIDDENHAM
BEDFORD
WILLINGTON
BEDFORD BOROUGH
WENSLEY
HATLEY
COPLE
CARDINGTON
KEMPSTON
ELSTOW
WIXAMTREE
WRESTLINGWORTH
NORTHILL
SUTTON
EYEWORTH
WOOTTON
BIGGLESWADE
DUNTON
REDBORNSTOKE
WARDEN
BIGGLES-WADE
WILSHAMSTEAD
HAYNES
SOUTHILL
EDWORTH
CRANFIELD
MARSTON
LANGFORD
HOUGHTON
SALFORD
HULCOTE
LIDLINGTON
CLIFTON
ASTWICK
CLOPHILL
CAMPTON
ARLESEY
MAULDEN
STOTFOLD
(HERTS)
CLIFTON
MILLBROOK
AMPTHILL
MEPPERSHALL
GRAVENHURST
HENLOW
HUSBORNE CRAWLEY
RIDGMONT
SEGENHOE
STEPPINGLEY
FLITWICK
FLITTON
STONDON
FLITT
SHILLINGTON
ASPLEY
PULLOXHILL
WOBURN
HIGHAM
WESTON (HERTS)
EVERSHOLT
TINGRITH
POTSGROVE
MILTON
HARLINGTON
BARTON
MANSHEAD
STAN-BRIDGE
BATTLESDEN
TODDINGTON
SUNDON
STREATLEY
CHALGRAVE
HOCKLIFFE
LEIGHTON
ROYAL LAND
TILS-WORTH
HOUGHTON REGIS
ROYAL
LAND
EATON
STAN-BRIDGE
CADDINGTON
LUTON
KENSWORTH
FLITT
WHIPSNADE
STUDHAM

The old oak tree on which Abbot Hobbs is said to have been hanged, as it is today. On it a plaque reads: 'Robert Hobbs, the last Abbot of the Monastery was tried by Jury at Woburn for Treason on June 14th, 1538. He was sentenced by the court to be taken to the gallows, THIS TREE, and hanged. Kings Bench Records, 540-271'. (JW)

John Russell, 1st Earl of Bedford. This engraving was used as a frontispiece in Jeremiah Wiffen's book about the Russell family. (MTTBE)

ABOVE: An aerial view of Woburn Abbey, with the village and church tower in the distance, before the east wing and riding schools were demolished. (CJR/SR)
BELOW: The east wing of the Abbey, demolished in the 1950s. (CJR/SR)

Many Mansions

For at least four hundred years the church in Woburn itself was just a chapel-of-ease to the now non-existent parish church of Birchmore. This parish was about a mile to the north of Woburn, but all that remains of it today is a farmhouse and a few cottages. The advowson (the right to 'present' a clergyman) of the parish church at Birchmore was part of Hugh de Bolebec's original gift when he founded the Abbey at Woburn in 1145, with the proviso that the Abbey should provide a competent priest. In 1308 the Abbot obtained a licence from the King to appropriate Birchmore and its tithes, and to use the glebe land (land that could be farmed by the incumbent). In 1363 a licence was granted by the Bishop for a monk to serve the cure for three years because of the poverty of the benefice and the scarcity of secular priests, and in 1399 a further licence for a monk to serve was obtained from the Pope. However, by 1526 a secular chaplain was receiving £4 a year for serving Birchmore with Dom Ralf Barnys as curate and, when Lord Russell received the manor of Woburn in 1547 with the parsonage of Birchmore, £10 was to be allowed for the salary of the priest serving Birchmore.

On a map of Woburn made by Sir Jonas Moore and dated 1661, the churchyard is marked, indicating that the church once stood about 200 yards from the present farmhouse, at the end of a field with the name of Hedgecroft, not far from Aspley Lane. The late Rev T.N. Gunner, a former vicar of Woburn, was flown over this site by the RAF:

'On Friday 7th November, 1952, at 1100 hours, I was flown over the site by the R.A.F. for the purpose of investigating this supposed site. In the field next but one to the Newport cottages on the way to Woburn Sands, I saw plainly the outline of a fairly large building. On visiting the field later on I found a clearly marked depression measuring approximately 105 feet by 75 feet facing east and west. Stake driving met hard substances about two feet below the surface.'

He goes on to say that a local archaeologist and a churchwarden assisted him with his investigations. Unfortunately there was neither a map nor drawing with his notes to show the exact site.

We do not know when Birchmore church finally disappeared. At the disolution, Birchmore was held by Edward Staunton and his son Robert as bailiffs for the Abbey. Since the Birchmore lands had once been Abbey lands, the Staunton family must have had either a grant or a lease of them before 1535. The ancient deed and charters of the Abbey have never been found and maybe the Stauntons concealed their lease of land including a meadow called Lord's Mead. This meadow, marked on the map of 1661, was adjacent to their own house and quite possibly they hid or took abbey documents as well as a piece of abbey land since they were not taken into the hands of the Crown at the time of the dissolution. Moore's 1661 survey says:

'Birchmore a pretended Mannor of Seigniory under Wooborne there is a faire howse with gardens and all convenient howses to it and very many pritty closes which were formerly Comon Feildes but by the Lord Francis Earle of Bedfordes favour Sir Francis Stanton enclosed and built the howse it cont. 100 acres.'

The house was probably built in or shortly after the reign of Queen Elizabeth I or a little later. Sir Francis Staunton was knighted by James I at Bletsoe in 1621 and was a benefactor to the people of Woburn. The last Staunton we know to have been at Birchmore was Staveley Staunton, who was buried in 1678. Birchmore eventually passed to the Pickering family (descendants by marriage of Staveley Staunton) and in 1747 the then Duke bought the lands from Sir Edward Pickering. In 1793 Holland produced plans to convert the old manor house into a farmhouse for about £1,600, later reduced to £1,100 and it may have undergone further changes since then.

It is not known when the chapel-of-ease was built in Woburn itself — such chapels were sometimes built in scattered parishes where the inhabitants had to come to church from a distance. However, it was there by 1242 when Henry III granted a weekly market to the Abbot to be held at the 'chapel of Old Woburn' (the abbey site would have been termed 'new' Woburn). By 1245 Woburn was a parochial church and was obviously a Rectory before 1302 when the last Rector was instituted. The *Liber Regis* in 1535 listed Birchmore and Woburn under separate headings, calling Birchmore a Vicarage and Woburn a perpetual curacy. Also in 1535, Abbot Hobbs is said by many books to have rebuilt the church at Woburn. Certainly in 1535 a Woburn man left 20d for 'bylding of the chapell of Woburne'. Sometimes Woburn people asked in their wills to be buried at Birchmore and sometimes at Woburn. In 1500 John Shyngleshurt asked in his will to be buried in Birchmore churchyard, left money to the church and 20d for the last payment for the great bell there. However, the inhabitants of Woburn would obviously have found the chapel-of-ease more convenient, especially if they lived in the south or west of the parish and, since there was a fairly marked rise in the population of Woburn during the 16th century, it is likely that Woburn's chapel would have become more popular. The parish church at Birchmore continued for some time, but tradition says that Sir Francis Staunton (who died in 1639) built or rebuilt the tower of the church at Woburn early in the 17th century using stones from the church at Birchmore.

We do not know what the now lost church at Birchmore or the original chapel-of-ease at Woburn looked like. However, if it is assumed that the old church and tower (standing in Bedford Street) described by Dodd in 1818 and Parry in 1831 were more or less the same as the 17th century buildings, then the tower stood about six yards from the main building, as it does today, fifty feet high. The buttresses were large and there was a pinnacle on each corner. On the roof was a large octagonal cupola (lantern) made of wood covered with lead, and on the top a cross and vane. Inside this open lantern was a Sanctus bell cast in 1637. On the eight pilasters which supported the lantern were the arms and ciphers of Abbot Hobbs, which were also to be found inside the church. Parry says that the church itself had always consisted of three aisles — a nave and north and south aisles — and a chancel, the nave being sixty feet long and the chancel thirty feet long. The general architecture appeared to be fifteenth century or a little later. There were four arches on each side 'very prettily moulded and of graceful sweep, and resting on octagonal pillars'. The chancel arch was higher and had clustered columns. There were several memorials. One of these was a fourteenth century brass effigy of a priest (the brass unfortunately missing) on a grey marble slab in the south aisle. According to Dodd, above the priest's head was a brass plate with a Latin inscription on it which he translated as 'Here lieth John Morton, formerly son of John Morton, of Pottesgrave, Lord of Lovelesbury; who died on the day of the Conversion of St Paul, in the year of our Lord one thousand three hundred and ninety-four. On whose soul may God have mercy.'

It was the fashion for those gentry who could afford it to put sculptured tombs in church and another memorial on the north wall of the chancel was an alabaster monument of ten figures in memory of Sir Francis Staunton (who died in 1639) and his wife who died in 1630. Above the figures was an inscription, now mostly erased, but given by Dodd in 1818 as 'Here lieth Sir Francis Staunton, Knight, who was High Sherife of this County; aged —, and dyed — ' (obviously erected by him and never completed after his death) 'And Dame Elizab. his Wife, aged 66 who, died in 1630.

> The mother's dead, father and sons survive,
> His grace must make them after death alive;
> When — though a golden name in marble sitt,
> Is ther a new name on the white stone writt
> In that alone will comfort then be found,
> When that God's angel the last trump doth sound.'

(The remains of the brass and the memorial are both in the present mortuary chapel).

A list of church goods in 1651 (the original now lost) shows the furniture and fittings to include:

'*Imprimis* One Church Bible; Item, one Book of Martyrs; one part of Bishop Jewell's Works; one Book of the Paraphrase of Erasmus upon the Gospels one Register Book in parchment; one Pulpit Cloth; one Hour Glass; one great pewter Flagon; one pewter-spouted Pot; one Communion Table Cloth of Linen; two Napkins; one Carpet Cloth for the Communion Table; one pewter Dish; one Gilt Cup and Cover, wrought with Gold; one silver Cup and Cover; two Boxes to gather money in; two Tables and Frames; one old Chest, bound with iron; one new Chest, with three locks; one other old Chest; two Fire Hooks and one Chain; one broken Fire Hook; Leathern Buckets; one Bearer (i.e. Bier); three sides of Rails for the Communion Table; three broken Bells with Clappers; one whole Bell; one iron Clock, with a Bell proper to it; one Saint's Bell; one Poor Man's Box.'

The churchwardens levied a rate on the whole parish and kept in repair not only the church but also the parish or town houses. They also repaired the parish butts (used for archery practice) and paid '. . . for Lyme to mend the Pavementes of the Church . . . for mending the Bell wheeles and grease for them . . . for a Bellrope . . . for glaseing of the Church windowes . . . for making of a form for the Church . . . for washing the Church Lynnen . . . for washing the surplisse twice . . . for making clean the leads . . . for boards for the seats in the Chauncell . . '. By 1671 Woburn had 163 houses and a population of about 720, so there should have been room for all the able-bodied in the church on Sundays.

Over the years the presence of the Russell family at the Abbey meant that there were many improvements and repairs to the building. About 1730 an iron clock was put into the tower with its face only about ten feet from the ground. It cost 20 guineas, one half of which was given by the Duke, the other half raised by public subscription. About 1750 John, 4th Duke, sought to improve the interior of the church by decorating the chancel with an elliptical arched roof 'richly ornamented with various bold carvings of flowers and cross ribs, supported by Roman corbels, in plaister of Paris . . .' (Parry) directed by Sir William Chambers. The Duke also put in a large east window which Dodd says formerly had coats of arms in it but in 1818 was 'in the simple Gothic style'. Two side windows were put in and the floor was relaid with squares of free-stone and black marble.

It was about this time that the Dukes of Bedford began to claim that Woburn was a peculiar, free from the interference of a bishop or archdeacon. The 1st Duke (1616-1700) leant strongly to nonconformity, and he and his successors based their claim on the fact that Cistercian religious houses had been exempt from the bishop's jurisdiction. Woburn itself was treated as a perpetual curacy, and the Russell family had the right to nominate the curate; from the Reformation until the time of the 1st Duke the bishops and archdeacons had exercised their ordinary powers in Woburn. The Dukes never tried to take over the archdeacon's right to prove wills, but certainly between 1755 and 1762 they granted marriage licences. However, this dispute ended with the abolition of all peculiar jurisdictions in 1857. Probably because he considered himself free from episcopal control, in 1796 Francis, 5th Duke, who could not bear the 'Benedicite' at Morning Prayer, had books of Common Prayer for the parish church printed without it.

At the end of the 18th century Francis, 5th Duke, thoroughly repaired the church. Two new galleries were put in at the west end of the aisles to accommodate the Sunday Schools; these were 'in addition to the handsome centre one which bears the stamp of antiquity'. The old pulpit in the 'florid Gothic style, finely carved with niches etc.' was replaced by a 'modern' one made from oak which was erected in the centre of the church. New pews were also bought. The pews were of the old 'horse box' type and the privileged who sat in them had to pay for them. The pewing of the church was partly paid for by the Duke of Bedford and a portion was charged on the seat owners and holders of property in the town — the number was sometimes noted on the deeds of shop or house. The poorer classes had to either sit on benches or stand in the aisles. These renovations also included a reorganisation of the churchyard, which occasioned the churchwardens to put an advertisement in a local newspaper on 7 May 1801 informing friends and relations of persons interred in the churchyard.

During the 18th century there was a widespread reintroduction of music into church services. Music in the church at Woburn seems to have followed the national trend. There were no hymns in the prayer book and organs had been discarded long ago, so music first returned for metrical versions of the psalms. Initially these were sung unaccompanied, a pitch-pipe being used to give the singers the first note. Gradually, however, small bands came into use consisting usually of oboe, clarinet and bassoon, and the instrumentalists and singers performed from a gallery in the church. At Woburn the churchwardens' accounts record that a new bassoon was purchased in 1760 and, in 1767, 6s 6d was paid for '4 Bassoon Reeds and Carriage of ditto'. In 1801 one guinea was paid for a 'Trumpet top to the bassoon' with 4s for reeds and in 1808 'William Gresham repairing Clarrinett 10s'. By 1789 there was a choir: 'Candles for Singers in the church 7s 5d' and in 1811 and 1812 the churchwardens paid 'John Hendley for teaching the Boys to sing £1 6s'. However, when there were no performers, or they were considered inadequate, an alternative was to install a barrel-organ. A barrel purchased for the barrel-organ from Messrs Flight and Robson on 25 September 1814 for £12 8s 6d spelt doom for the church band, and caused much ill feeling which was the subject of some correspondence between William Harland, leader of the musicians, and Robert Salmon, the Duke's steward and a churchwarden. There had been complaints 'That the flutes used did not chord well together' despite tuning before Divine Service William Harland explains 'perhaps it is not known that one Flute sometimes takes the tenor part while another plays the canto or treble and consequently strikes a different sound. They were ordered not to use flutes and were left with a clarinet and a bass viol which could not provide so much harmony'. They therefore 'retire from the Gallery with feelings of pleasure mingled with regret — pleasure for attempting to secure the approbation of the Community and to increase the attendance of the Public at Church . . . many prefer the Wind Instruments to the Organ' and regret 'that we have not found in Woburn (tho' inhabited by so respectable a body of Gentlemen) one person to step forward to give us the least Encouragement in . . . our laudable undertaking'. In his reply Robert Salmon says that the part taken by him as churchwarden 'has been by express command of the Duke of Bedford'. 'Your instruments were considered discordant and disapproved of by His Grace and that . . . perhaps a Clarinet with the Base Viol would be sufficient and less objectionable, altho His Graces opinion is that the Instruments are altogether improper . . . I especially feel inclined in any matter to render the Church Service attractive and with pleasure regard Your efforts to that end but I have not heard any of the Inhabitants express their preference of instruments to the Organ.'

Improvements and additions continued through the 19th century. John, 6th Duke, presented the church with a painting of *The Virgin and Child* by Carlo Maratti which was to be used as an altar piece. The old altar, described by Parry as 'in the Roman style, and lofty, with a pediment' was therefore replaced in 1811 by a smaller one with Gothic panelling designed so that the Maratti painting fitted the centre panel.

In 1811 the Duke also gave to the church some silver gilt communion plate consisting of two chalices, two patens and two alms plates made in London in 1762. A new east window was put in of a perpendicular Gothic style, of five lights with cinquefoil arched mullions. It was fitted with stained glass. A new stove was also installed. The 1811 restoration was directed by the architect Sir William Chambers and cost between £1,200 and £1,500. A few years earlier, in about 1808, Georgina, wife of John the 6th Duke, had asked for ivy to be planted round the church and by 1818 this had grown to such an extent that Dodd says, 'The church presents a dignified and venerable appearance, being nearly covered with ivy . . . and it has in many places over-topt the battlements'.

In 1820 the old font was removed by the churchwardens and a 'silver Christianity bowl' was bought for 6 guineas to replace it. However, it was not used for long because in 1830 Sir Hugh Hoare, Bt, of Wavendon, gave a marble basin that was placed in the chancel.

1830 saw the rebuilding of the tower. The 6th Duke was employing the architect Edward Blore on other buildings in the town and asked him to redesign the church tower. The churchwardens' accounts for 12 May 1829 record 'Gave the Workmen on Laying first Stone of the new Tower of the Church for a supper etc. £1 (The Duke of Bedford gave the Like)'. The tower was rebuilt from the lower storey upwards; its height was increased to a total of 92 feet and an octagonal stone lantern was put on the top. The tower was now joined to the north aisle by a vestry and gallery which had two small windows. Parry (1831) comments that this had been the case once before when the parish clerk lived in an appartment 'supported by an arch which joined the tower to the church' but this had been pulled down before the 19th century. A new clock was presented by the Duke and the clock face, set in a square tablet, was placed higher up under the eastern belfry window — where it is today. A brass plate on the clock has the inscription: 'Erected in the tower of Woburn church by John, Duke of Bedford, 1830. Made by B.L. Vulliamy. London. No. 1087. Clockmaker to the King'.

In 1836 the Duke presented a new organ to the church. On 18 May 1836 it was recorded 'Thanks to the Duke of Bedford for his present of an organ — he to nominate an organist'. Mrs Castleden was appointed organist at a salary of £15 'for the present year' with John Hendley as organ blower at a salary of £4 per annum. (He had previously been paid £1 6s in 1813 for attending the organ and teaching the boys to sing). On 28 March 1839 a Mr Brown was appointed organist at £30 a year, 'he be subject to the control of the minister as to the number of verses etc. which he plays'.

There was apparently a large chandelier in the church 'that was often cleaned'; the church was lit by candles and oil lamps until about 1850, when gas was used.

The patronage, taste and money of the family at the Abbey meant that the church was quite exceptional for such a small community. However, there was an anonymous columnist who contributed articles signed 'W.A.' to local newspapers in the 1840s and 1850s. Each article took one local church and criticised the fittings, architecture and upkeep. The letters 'W.A.' stood for Woburn Abbey and the columnist was the 7th Duke's librarian, John Martin. Surely, without the sympathy of his employer, he could hardly have published the following on 31 January 1846 as a description of a church largely built, furnished and decorated by the Duke's ancestors:

'BEDFORDSHIRE CHURCHES, No. 22. WOBURN. The exterior of this church deserves every commendation; the same praise cannot be bestowed upon the interior, where Christian and Pagan architecture are strangely jumbled together. This chiefly prevails in the roofs of the chancel and nave. The ceiling of the aisles is of the ordinary sort. It is lamentable to see space sacrificed to the system of pews; there are only a few free seats in the nave. The position of the reading desk and pulpit is most absurd, and compels the chief part of the congregation to be seated with their backs to the altar. It is scarcely possible to create a more palpable blemish than that which is occasioned by placing the pulpit in the centre of the nave. In a dissenting meeting house, it may be proper to assign this station to the preacher, but it is quite inconsistent with the intent of our liturgy, and should never be tolerated. The situation of the reading-desk, below the pulpit, like the desk of an auctioneer's clerk, is equally inappropriate.

'A number of common-looking lamps disfigure as well as blacken with their smoke the walls of the building; this is one result of abandoning the custom of the English church by changing the afternoon into an evening service; when lighted up the church presents a very theatrical appearance. The organ excludes the light from the west window of the nave, and a miserable gallery stretches across four other windows in this part of the church; if open seats were substituted for the pews, this gallery might be removed. The floor of the latter was strewed, when we visited it, with a quantity of nutshells. The font is as much out of character as out of place. W.A.'

In the middle of the 19th century the population of Woburn grew to some 2,000 and although there were a few free seats for the poor, a great many people soon found themselves unable to get into the church to attend services. The Dukes of Bedford once more took on the responsibility for the church building. William, 8th Duke, commissioned the architect Henry Clutton to design a new and much larger church for the same site. Clutton was a national figure who did much work for the Russell family. Among other buildings of his in the county are the churches of Steppingley, Souldrop and Woburn Sands, all villages where the Russell family had influence. He also designed the Park House (now Shuttleworth College) at Old Warden for the Shuttleworth family.

When rumour spread around the town of what the Duke had in mind, the townsfolk were far from happy. However, they were accustomed to the Duke directing and paying for the upkeep of the church so they could not disagree openly. Eventually a vestry meeting was called in the Town Hall, the Duke's representative explained what was intended and a resolution was passed tendering 'respectfull and greatful thanks for the great boon the Duke proposed to bestow on the inhabitants of the town'. So, on 17 April 1864 it was announced:

'That the present Parish Church of Woburn not affording sufficient accommodation for the Inhabitants, and more especially for the Poor, and being otherwise inconvenient, His Grace the Duke of Bedford, had been pleased to signify his intention, on the request of the Parishioners, to entirely rebuild the church on the present site.'

The cost was estimated to be £10,246 3s, the whole to be defrayed by the Duke.

Demolition of the old church began on 13 June 1864, but it was soon found that the new building could not be erected to the plans and specifications without 'objectionable disturbance of the graves of deceased parishioners'. Another vestry meeting was therefore called, on 27 October 1864, and a letter from the Duke was read, expressing his willingness to grant a new site for the parish church of Woburn, provided that the parishioners preferred it to the old one. 'Thereupon it was unanimously resolved that the offer of His Grace the Duke of Bedford be accepted.' Two faculties were therefore applied for and granted. One was for the pulling down of the old church and the building of a mortuary chapel: 'for the performance of the Burial Service according to the Liturgy of the United Church of England and Ireland, over the Bodies and Persons dying Inhabitants of the said Parish'. The second faculty was for the erection of a new church on a new site.

And so the buildings which stand today on the site of the old chapel-of-ease in Woburn High Street are the tower of 1830 (with some old stone identifiable at its base, probably taken from the former parish church of Birchmore by Sir Francis Staunton in the early 17th century) and the Mortuary Chapel which was built in 1865.

In the Mortuary Chapel itself may be seen certain items from the old church. The alabaster monument to the Staunton family is on the north wall and the remains of the 14th century brass is in the south-east corner. A marble tablet is on the east wall as you enter with the inscriptions: 'In the year 1865, William, 8th Duke of Bedford, built this chapel on the site and from the materials of the parish church'. It would seem that some of the glass from the east window of the old church was used in the east window of the Mortuary Chapel, for the figures in the upper part are the same. The general design of the stonework is also the same, but the overall length of the window is considerably shorter than that of the old church window.

It is thought that the organ from the old church was put into Eversholt church. The organ there bears a plate with the inscription 'The gift of John, Duke of Bedford, 1836', it has the name Snetsler inside it and there is also evidence that a barrel mechanism was once fitted to it.

For a time eight 'hatchments' hung round the walls of the Mortuary Chapel. They apparently used to hang in round recesses on the walls of the old church.

They are not hatchments in the true sense of the word and are probably more correctly referred to as 'commemorative armorial plates'. They are large, circular, painted on wood and all appear to have been painted at the same time. The background design is the same on each one, only the shield of arms being different. The dates painted on the shields range from 1086 to 1781. However, these 'hatchments' were moved to the present church in 1977 for safekeeping as the Mortuary Chapel fell into disuse. In November 1981 the Mortuary Chapel was officially declared a redundant building. Although plans have been proposed and considered for its restoration and upkeep, at the time of writing its future is still in doubt.

The old church was demolished in 1864 and the small Mortuary Chapel was built on the site in 1865, but the new parish church was not completed until 1868. The Duke therefore provided a temporary building of wood for use as a church until the new one was finished. It had a nave, chancel, two aisles and room for 750 people. When it was no longer needed at Woburn the Duke gave it to the Vicar of Luton for use as a Mission Church in a district of his parish called High Town, where St Matthew's church was later built.

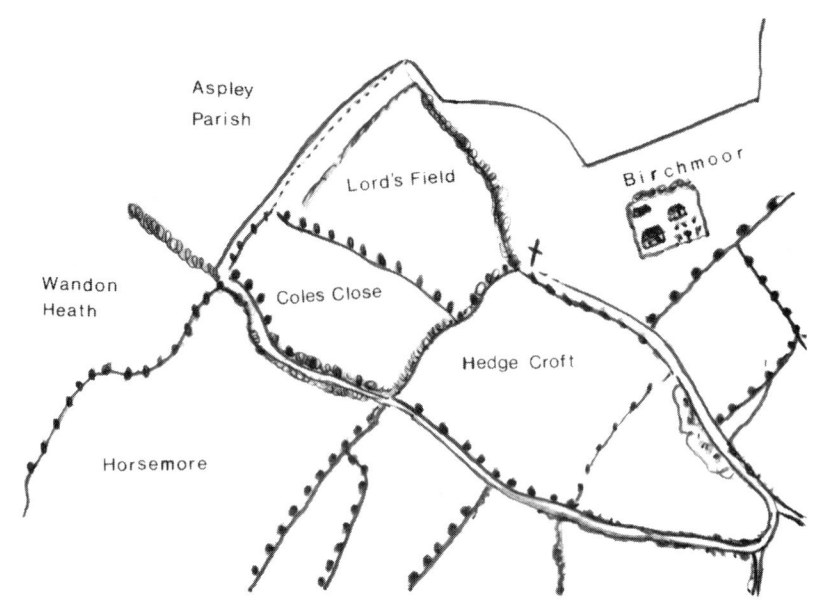

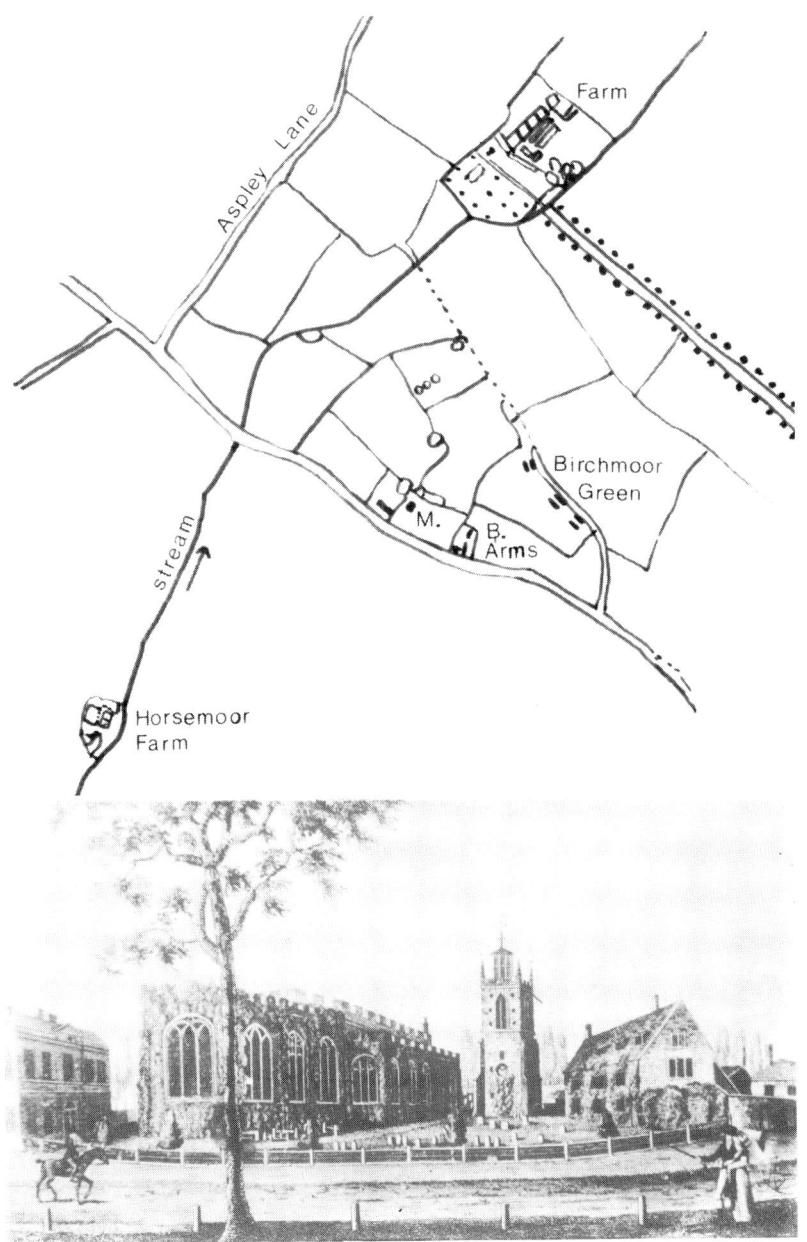

Sketch maps of Birchmore; OPPOSITE ABOVE; based on an original map by Sir Jonas Moore in 1661, and ABOVE: on a 19th century ordnance survey map; (A) OPPOSITE BELOW: all that is Birchmore today, besides a farmhouse. (A) BELOW: The old church c1818, viewed from the east; the old parsonage is on the left and the school on the right. (SD)

39

ABOVE: The old church c1818 viewed from the west. The lantern on the tower was made of wood but by 1829 was so decayed that it was replaced with the present one of stone. Woburn school, founded in 1582, is on the left. (BCRO) BELOW: The old church and tower, probably taken in the early 1860s. Written on the back: 'This photo was taken of my Father and Mother when he was a curate at Woburn to Mr Cumberledge — and my eldest brother John . . . J.L.D.S'. Rev Cumberledge was incumbent 1856-1874, followed by Henry Willes Southey, 1874-1900 — presumably the man in the photo. (CJR/SR)

WOBURN, 7th May, 1801.

THE CHURCHWARDENS of WOBURN, in Bedfordshire, hereby inform the Public, and particularly the Friends and Relations of Persons interred in the Parish-Church and Church-Yard of WOBURN aforesaid, that the said Church is now under a thorough Repair, and is intended to be new pewed after the Floor has been raised with Soil taken from the high and uneven Parts of the *Church-Yard*, so as to bring the same to an even and regular Surface, intended to be sown anew with Grass, in Order that it may hereafter be kept clean and neat: The said Church-yard being so much filled with Grave-Stones, Grave-Rails, and Arches turned with Brick over the Graves of Persons long since buried, that there is not sufficient Burial-Room for the present Extent of the Town. It is proposed in levelling the Church-Floor and Church-Yard, to remove such Grave-Stones, Grave-Rails, and Brick-work, of fifteen Years standing and upwards (using the Stones afterwards in new Paving the Church-Floor) except of such Persons whose Relations or Friends shall on or before the first Day of next Month, (June, 1801,) point out to one of the said Churchwardens the particular Grave, Rail, or Stone, they may wish to have preserved, and pay down the Expence which will attend the re-fixing of the same after the Church-Floor and Surface of the Church-Yard are brought to their proper Levels.

J. FAREY.
THO. SHAW.

LEFT: The alabaster Staunton family memorial, erected by Sir Francis Staunton before he died in 1639. In 1864 the memorial was removed and then placed in its present position in 1865. (JW/V) RIGHT: The newspaper entry in 1801 regarding alterations to the churchyard. (JDP) BELOW: The clock in the old church tower. It was made by Benjamin Louis Vulliamy, clockmaker to William IV, given by John, 6th Duke, in 1830, and is still working today. (JW/V)

The painting of *The Virgin and Child* by Carlo Maratti (1625-1713). (JW/V)

LEFT: A view inside the old church c1860, showing the painting of *The Virgin and Child* by Maratti behind the altar. One of the recesses in which the hatchments hung can be seen on the left, the pews are boxed and the lighting appears to be by gas. (JW/V) RIGHT: The east window of the old church given by John, 6th Duke, in 1811. (JDP) BELOW: The mortuary chapel and old church tower today. (JW)

43

LEFT: The clock bell which still strikes the hour and was the 7th of the ring of eight that hung in the old tower. (JW/V) RIGHT: The wrought iron gate at the base of the old church tower which gives entry to the mortuary chapel. The old stonework surrounding the archway is thought to be from the old church at Birchmore, brought to its present site by Francis Staunton. (A) BELOW: A view today looking east inside the mortuary chapel. (JW/V)

A view from the west side of the old church tower and mortuary chapel, showing the tower of the present parish church in the distance. (CJR/SR)

19th century map of Woburn Town, Abbey and Park.

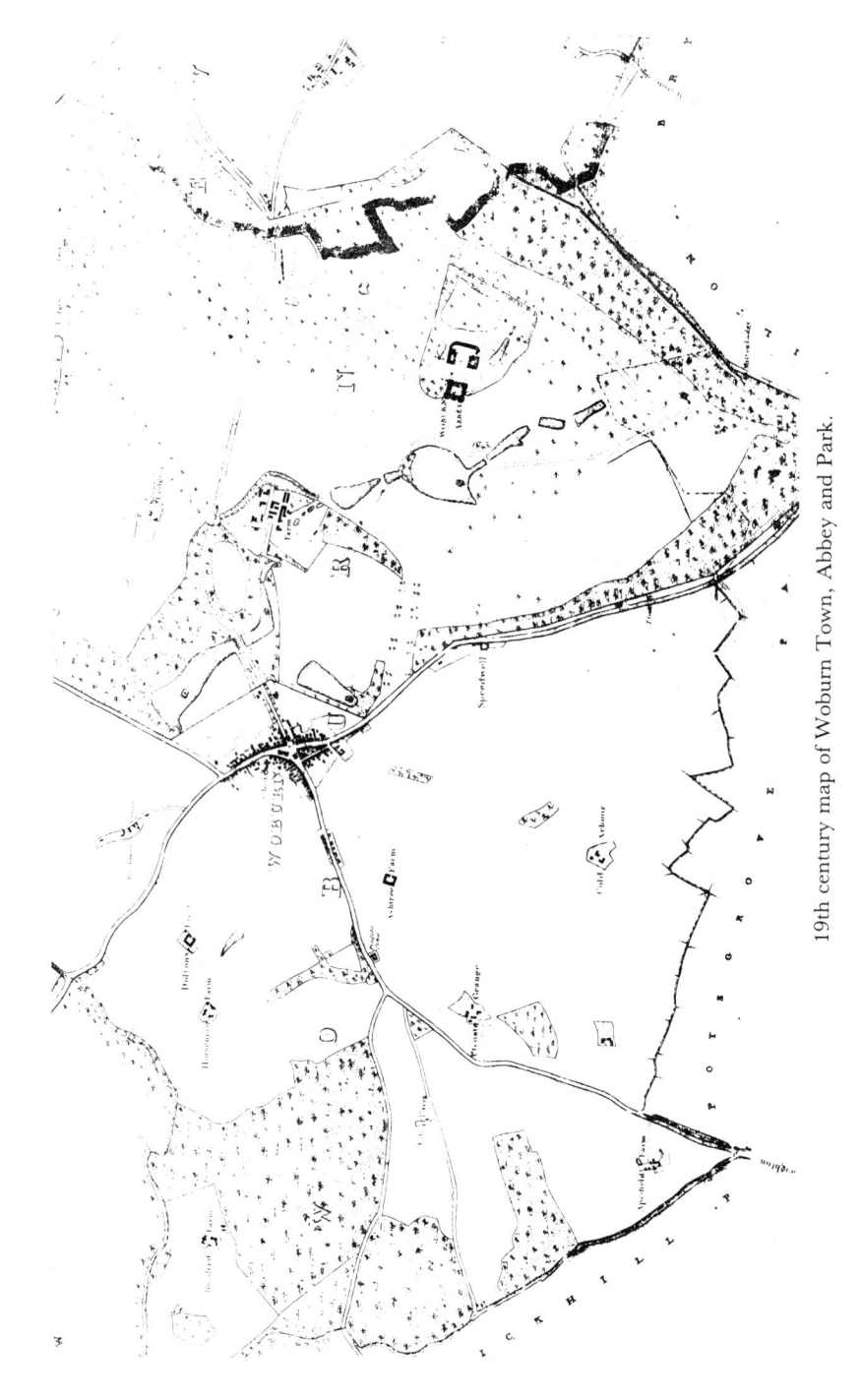

Private Means and Public Works

The early settlement at Woburn would seem to have been little more than a hamlet to the main parish of Birchmore. However, the founding of the monastery in 1145 and its needs soon brought increased traffic and trade such that the centre of activity shifted and Birchmore declined while Woburn prospered. The granting of a weekly market and annual fair in 1242 and two more fairs in 1530 indicates that the community was growing in size and importance, and was becoming a thriving market town.

The right to hold markets was granted by the King, and from early times weekly markets disposed locally of surplus goods and made up deficiencies. They were usually held on a Sunday, but gradually weekday markets became general and Woburn's market granted by Henry III was on Fridays. On market days Woburn was so crowded that traffic travelling from Ampthill to Leighton Buzzard used to by-pass the town by using the bridle-way between the Almshouses (now Staunton House) and Gas Lane near the old Pound.

A fair was also granted by the King and was a bigger occasion, bringing traders from as far afield as London with goods which were not easy to get locally, such as iron, gold, silver and brass. There was also trading in horses and other livestock. Woburn's three-day fair was granted in 1242 for 14 September, the Feast of the Holy Cross. Of the other fairs granted in 1530 by Henry VIII, one was held in March, at which many horses, cattle and sheep were sold, and the other, the Cherry Fair, was held in July. A Statty or Hiring Fair was later held in October, bringing roundabouts or a circus and towards the end of last century the type of entertainment expected at a fair today. According to some 19th century commercial directories a fair in January was also added. Everyone was free to attend the markets and fairs and beer would not have been lacking. Details of incidents, which probably resulted from this, can be found in court records; Sir Thomas Fermbaud, six times MP for Bedfordshire, was concerned in a brawl at Woburn Fair in 1334. Pick-pockets were also prevalent and in 1671 a Surrey woman stole bone lace at Woburn fair, concealing it in the crown of her hat. In the same year Mary Williamson stole pewter flagons from inns in Ampthill, removed the innkeeper's marks and offered them for sale at Woburn, while in 1684 Richard Gaseley, a Woburn upholsterer, was found making up 20 yards of material which had been stolen from Robert Perrot's shop in Leighton Buzzard.

In 1290 the cortège bearing the body of Edward's wife, Queen Eleanor, rested overnight in the town on its journey from Grantham to Westminster Abbey. Crosses were erected in every place where the cortège had stopped on its journey, to perpetuate the Queen's memory. The Woburn cross was built in 1292, a little later than most, on what is now known as Market Square. A great part of the work was done by Ralph de Chichester at a cost of £60 6s 8d. Unfortunately the cross has long since disappeared.

On the Market Square stands the present Town Hall. The original Town Hall, or Market House, was built in 1737. It had three floors, the upper rooms were used for public meetings, concerts, petty sessions and other business of the town; the ground floor had a cloister aisle, open to the air, with ironwork fitments which were used by butchers on market days, and the basement was used mainly as a wine store. A large cupola topped with a gilt vane was on the roof at one end and housed a bell which was used as a fire warning. However, this building was pulled down in 1830. The bell was taken to Park Farm in Woburn Park, from where it was later stolen. John, 6th Duke, employed Edward Blore to design the new Town Hall. Blore was architect to King William IV and Queen Victoria and designed the frontage of Buckingham Palace. In Woburn he worked on other projects for the Duke, rebuilding the church tower and designing the house which became the second parsonage. In 1831 Parry described the Town Hall as 'of the latest Gothic: the sides have each four cloister arches, filled with iron work: at the east end is a neat arched doorway, over which is a handsome oriel window; there are also two stone wyverns at the eaves of the roof, and the north east angle has a square tower, with a spiral leaded roof and vane . . . the edifice also includes the watch-house, which was formerly an octagonal building, with a lantern, in the small square behind the Market-house'.

building was restored and the interior refitted, under the direction of Henry Clutton, by Hastings, 9th Duke of Bedford. A new door and porch to the west front were added in 1912 by Herbrand, 11th Duke. Nearly a century later, in 1974 the Marquess of Tavistock restored it yet again, converting the ground floor into offices and making an upper floor as a hall for recreation purposes. The architects were Donald W. Insall and Associates.

According to Dodd, behind the Town Hall lay a small square in the centre of which was a 'commodious watch-house, surmounted by a lantern'. Although there was a town watchman he says there were few street lamps in 1818, but according to the records David Whitman was paid £4 18s 1d for lighting the lamps in 1810.

A bell man or town crier used to sweep the streets, for the churchwardens' accounts record that in 'April 1770, 1 doz. Broomes to Bellman 1s 6d'. A town crier was listed in a Commercial Directory as recently as 1914 when it was Francis Keens of London Road (now incorporated into George Street) who was a 'bill poster and town crier'.

There were two 'Drovers' Ponds' or watering places in Woburn. Only one of these remains, though not used, called Pinfold Pond. It stands south of the road, about 100 yards beyond 'Maryland' travelling to Leighton Buzzard. The other was at the north end of the town, next to the almshouses, where a house now stands opposite the turning to Husborne Crawley.

Stray cattle were held in a pound until claimed by the owners. The pound still exists along Leighton Street at Gas Lane. Its dilapidated state was put in good order in 1932 and at least once more since, but it is again in need of repair. The key labelled 'Woburn Pound Sept. 20, 1879' and the padlock dated 1800 used to be kept in a glass fronted case in the Town Hall, for if your beast was locked in the pound, a fine had to be paid before you could take it away.

The town also used to have a Cage for locking up people who misbehaved. Moore's survey of 1661 says 'CADGE HOWSE this stands at Leighton lane's end in the midst of the Streete nere Irelands tenement cont. two bayes of building is in bad repair. On the east side standes the Cadge and Stocks'. The parish kept it in repair and provided a lamp. Records of assizes and quarter sessions show that it was in steady use from at least 1671 — in 1823 difficulty was apparently experienced in getting a drunken man into it.

In 1836 the Woburn Mechanics Institute was established and was merged into the Woburn Literary and Scientific Institution in 1850. This was housed in the upper room of the Town Hall and had a library of 2,000 books, daily and weekly newspapers, anatomical charts, maps, and scientific specimens displayed in cases. Lectures and concerts were held there and a show about Arctic regions, using the new 'magic lantern', was given in 1868. A triennial exhibition was held from 1850 to the 1870s. At the restoration of the Town Hall in 1884 the Institute moved to Leighton Street into a reading room which had been converted from some shops in 1883. The lending library continued and there was a games room, but after the Second World War it was closed, mainly because of lack of support. The library and billiards table were sold, valuable books only fetching a few pence and the premises became a hairdresser's.

Over the centuries Woburn has owed much to the patronage of the Abbey. Not until the time of the 4th Earl did the Russell family make a permanent home at Woburn. However, before this the house and the town did feature in the lives of the Russells from time to time. In 1560 Margaret St John, wife of Francis, 2nd Earl, died of smallpox at the Abbey and in 1572 Francis entertained Queen Elizabeth I there at her request. It was not a visit he welcomed for he wrote to Lord Burleigh: 'I am now going to prepare for her Majesty's coming to Woburne, which shall be done in the best and hartiest manner that I can. I trust your lordship will have in remembraunce to provide and helpe that her Majesty's tarrying be not above two nights and a day; for so long tyme do I prepare.'

Indeed, he even had to borrow plate and furniture to host her in the appropriate manner.

It was Francis, strongly Protestant and in favour of the new learning, who founded a Grammar school at Woburn, which still stands near the old church tower. On 5 July 1582 a piece of land 58' long and 26' wide 'on which a house for a free school is erected' was conveyed to trustees by the Earl. He also drew up 'Statutes for the Schoole at Woborne' which stated that the trustees were to nominate the schoolmaster who was to be between the ages of 26 and 50 and a 'Graduate haveing dexterite in teachinge and skilfull as well to make a verse as to writt in Prosse'. He was to be in school every day from 6 to 11 in the morning and again in the afternoon from 1 to 5 in winter and 1 to 6 in the summer. He must not allow more than one half-day holiday a week and that should not be on market or fair days. No pupil was admitted until he could read English well enough to be ready to learn 'Grammer' (Latin). On admission each boy paid 4d which was used to buy a Bible or other books 'to be cheyned upon deskes for the common use of the schollers'. Boys boarding in the town had to attend school on Sundays and Holy days before morning and evening service, to be catechised and hear readings on the principles of religion, after which 'they shall come orderlie to the church after the Scholemaister'. Morning and evening prayers, which were said daily, were put up on the schoolroom walls. A document dated 1602 says that twelve scholars nominated by the trustees, minister and churchwardens from the poorest of the parish, were to be taught free. Other scholars from the parish were to pay 2s 6d a quarter while 'foreners to paie as they can aggree with the scholemaster'. Local people also gave support to the school. In June 1582 William Stanton of Eversholt in his will gave to the free school 'nowe buildinge att Wooburne a blacke cowe called Jenkins', and in November 1587 Joan Balls of Woburn left 20s a year for two years towards the schoolmaster's stipend and '13s 4d to the byenge of Scapula his Lexicon (dictionary) to continue and remayne in the Scholehouse of Ooburne for the benefitt of Schollers' as well as 40s 'toward the buyeng of the Book of Marters which I would should be chayned to some convenyent place of the Church of Ooburne for the publique benefitt of the towne'. Joan Balls' will was witnessed by Humfrey Hill, schoolmaster.

Only a few children (boys) received education then. Sometimes poor children were taught to make lace in 'schools' run by the parish's two Overseers of the Poor so that it could be sold to earn money for the family. Pillow lace was first heard of in the north-east of the county at Eaton Socon but, by the 17th century, it was most strongly established in the west and spreading into Buckinghamshire. There is record of Woburn children being taught lace in 1618.

The 2nd Earl had intended the Free School to be a grammar school, teaching Latin and Greek in preparation for entry to university. However, in 1671 Woburn's population is estimated to have been 727, and a town as small as this could have provided only a few boys for whom this kind of education was suitable. By the 18th century therefore the school had become an ordinary charity school, and between 1708-1722 there were 30 boys who were clothed by the Duke at Whitsuntide every year — bills exist from this time for 30 coats, 30 pairs of breeches and 60 shirts and bands, together with caps, stockings, shoes and buckles. Thomas Gurney (1705-70) was schoolmaster for a time and invented the system of shorthand that bears his name. The Duchess apparently opened a private charity school of her own for poor girls, where 15 girls were clothed and taught how to knit, sew and work samplers. A bill exists for knitting needles and sampler materials supplied to the school, dated 1721. The Duchess died in 1724 but her mother, Mrs Elizabeth Howland, appears to have continued supporting the school. At least one sampler still survives, owned by a Woburn antique dealer. The text reads: 'In remembrance of the truly Honoured and Virtuous Lady Mrs Elizabeth Howland my good benefactour who in her life gave to ten children of this parish schooling and clothing books and samplars and by her last will and testament has left it to be continued for ever. She rest from her labours and her works do follow her. Please God bless his Grace the Duke and Duchess of Bedford and send them along to live for all their goodness unto me which I do receive'. Children were often instructed by their guardians to thank their benefactors in this way. The sampler ends with: 'Elisabeth Skilton wrought this in the 15 year of her age 1762'.

In 1808 the schoolhouse was repaired and the school reorganised under the Lancastrian system, whereby one master could instruct over a hundred children with the help of monitors. The school now had 104 boys who attended from 9-12 in the morning and 2-5 in the afternoon. They were instructed in eight classes by a monitor and his asistant, and their work was inspected by the Master. Writing was first practised on a 'Sand Desk', then on slates, and a copy-book was only allowed when a boy could do joined writing on a slate. Reading, spelling, elementary accounts and scripture were also part of the instruction. In 1814 the school was run by the British and Foreign Schools Society of which the then Duke was the first President. Girls' education at this time consisted of a Sunday School, where they could also learn to read, and later on in 1825 a school for girls was begun under the patronage of the Duke and Duchess of Bedford, in which instruction in needlework and Tuscan plait was also given. Parry says that in 1830, 137 boys and 63 girls were attending school. During the 19th century the population of Woburn was around 2,000, with a resultant increase in the number of school children. So, in 1845, new schools were built for 100 boys (in Leighton Street) and 120 girls (adjacent to the old school) while the old Free School building was used for infants. An Act of Parliament in 1870 introduced schooling everywhere and Woburn became a board school controlled by the ratepayers.

A school board was formed in 1873 and the Duke of Bedford leased the Free School to the board for an annual rent of 1s. This lease was later transferred to the Bedfordshire County Education Department. After 1928 children over 11 years had to attend other schools and, since 1978, the school has been a Lower school (5-11 years) in Bedfordshire's three-tier comprehensive system. At present there are about 40 pupils.

The old school used to have two floors, but the lower floor/ceiling was removed to heighten the rooms and so some of the original fireplaces are half-way up the walls! Above the upper and present ceiling/floor are the old dormitories, but they are inaccessible because there is now no staircase and as yet it has not been possible to work out where it originally was. In 1982 the school celebrated its 400th anniversary.

Standing in front of the school, and now part of it, is the old fire engine house. Fire-fighting was important to Woburn early on, for the town has suffered several large-scale fires. The first of which we have a detailed account was started on 13 September 1595 by a simple woman, who threw her old straw bedding onto the fire in her grate. Flames quickly swept up the chimney and through the whole house. Since most houses were roofed with thatch, which at the time was dry from a recent drought, and a strong breeze was blowing, the fire swiftly spread to destroy 130 houses. The townspeople did what they could and farmers even paid their men to help fight the inferno in the town. The inhabitants tried to save some of their possessions by placing them in the street, but these were looted and what little was left had either been burnt or damaged by water. A large store of goods for the September Fair was among the things destroyed.

The town was rebuilt, however, and prospered once more. We have some idea of trades in the town at that time from the way in which people described themselves in their wills, for by the 16th century the Parish Register in which occupations were noted was a legal obligation. Not only were there the usual trades which one might expect to find in any village such as butcher, baker, shoemaker and blacksmith, but also the more specialised services, for example draper, glover, weaver, horse collarmaker, joiner, brewer and innholder.

Lying on a main road, Woburn was on the routes of opposing forces during the Civil War. The town itself was generally Parliamentarian. However Prince Rupert and the Earl of Essex passed through in 1643 and Charles I stayed at the Abbey at least twice, once in 1645 and again two years later as a prisoner of Parliament. As a result of hostilities, Woburn suffered yet another fire but since the account of it was published in a Parliamentarian paper it may not be entirely objective! In November 1645 Royalist mounted troops, travelling from Oxford, stayed overnight at Leighton Buzzard and early the next morning moved on towards Woburn. Four young men of Woburn mounted their horses, went to meet them, exchanged shots and returned. The King's troops eventually entered Woburn in good order but were attacked by the people, so they retreated and returned later in the day with reinforcements. A battle followed during which the Major who commanded the Royalist troops was killed. After this there was no discipline and the troops ran riot. The town was plundered and set on fire, destroying at least 27 houses 'being all that side of the town which lies towards Newport Pagnell unto the church, the steeple whereof was burnt, but quickly quenched'. Parry says that during a Royalist raid in June 1644 'Birchmore House then in the occupance of Robert Staunton, was plundered, and had been more than once plundered before.'

At the Restoration, the 5th Earl of Bedford rode in the procession that welcomed Charles II on his return, but generally he took little part in public life. He was Protestant and had a nonconformist tutor, Rev John Thornton for his six sons and three daughters who, like their father, were strongly anti-papist. The second son, Lord William Russell was strongly against the Roman Catholic influence at court but was apparently not as prudent as his father, for he became implicated in the Rye House plot, was brought to trial, found guilty, and executed at Lincoln's Inn Fields on 21 July 1683. The family grief was naturally intense and William's wife, Rachel, worked relentlessly to prove her husband's innocence. She was successful in 1689, when William and Mary came to the throne, for Parliament passed an Act whereby the judgement on William Russell was reversed. The honour of the family was cleared and in 1694 the 5th Earl was given a Dukedom, becoming the 1st Duke of Bedford by way of recompense for his son's execution.

The third town fire was in 1724 when 39 houses were destroyed; as Dodd wrote in 1818 'The town soon rose, like a Phoenix from its ashes, with additional lustre; proving in this, as in many other instances, that misfortune, instead of a curse, frequently turns out a blessing'.

The first mention we have of a fire engine is in the Churchwardens' accounts of 1755. The engine was apparently frequently in need of repair and in 1778 was even taken to London for this purpose. It was also sent out to neighbouring parishes, for on Christmas Eve 1763 'Beer for the Men when the Fire was at Potsgrave and other Work Men. 5s 9d'. An engine house was built in front of the old Tudor school building in Bedford Street and for more than a century the engine and its house were under the control of the Churchwardens. A key for the Market House was purchased in 1765 for 18s 7d, presumably for quick access to ring the bell in a cupola on the roof used as a fire bell. The parish also had a supply of leather fire buckets and a town ladder (mended in 1767 for 2s 6d). H. Morrison, a journalist and local historian, writing in 1948 at the age of 80, recalled the 'ado' in getting into action the horses to draw the engine and the men in their wooden-topped helmets from various parts of the town and park. Herbrand, 11th Duke, (1858-1940) gave a steam engine to the town in place of the old manual one, but the cost of repair was apparently so great that it was returned to him. However, wartime brought the National Fire Service with a modern tender, trailer-pump and appliances and after representations, the new Duke, Hastings, built a new fire station in Leighton Street, at its junction with London End, and opened it himself in May 1947. It still stands and has up-to-date equipment, a loud siren and is run by the County Fire Service. The old engine house still stands in Bedford Street but has been taken over by the school and at present contains a cloakroom and the headmistress's study.

Besides war, the 17th century brought with it other miseries in the form of disease. Indeed, it was the plague which in effect caused the Abbey to become the permanent home of the Russell family. It was raging in London when, in August 1625, Francis Russell asked his cousin Edward, 3rd Earl of Bedford, for the loan of Woburn Abbey so that he, his wife and 10 children, who were then living in Chiswick, could seek refuge.

Market towns on main roads were vulnerable but the Abbey was well away from the town. The Russells escaped unharmed, but in the autumn there were more than 20 deaths from the plague in Woburn, including schoolmaster James Tong and five of his children, Michael Parratt and his wife and child, and six members of the Albrett family. In all, Woburn lost 50 people from the plague in 1625-26 and 40 in 1665.

Francis Russell succeeded his cousin as 4th Earl of Bedford two years later and decided to make Woburn his main country residence. The family liked the house and the surrounding country, but the building was in quite a bad state of repair because it had not been lived in for nearly 100 years, so much of it had to be rebuilt. Francis was less fortunate in avoiding another scourge of the time, for he died of smallpox in London in 1641.

The Staunton family, who had been stewards and bailiffs for the abbots and owned a small estate at Birchmore, were also benefactors to the town. As well as building the old church tower and erecting a family memorial in the old church (now in the Mortuary Chapel), Sir Francis Staunton provided for the poor in his will in 1635. An entry in the charities of the parish records runs: 'Sir Francis Staunton of this Parish by Will Dated 29th May 1635 did bequeath Forty Pounds to Purchase Estates for the benefit of the Poor which Sum by his Executors was on the 3rd October 1661 Vested in Certain other Lands and Tenements for the use and Benefit of the poor of the Parish . . .'.

An Act of 1760 granted these to John, 4th Duke of Bedford, on condition that he built and kept in repair twelve almshouses for poor families and provided £30 a year for their use. This was to be charged on the house and lands of Birchmore. There were then 20 inmates. In 1964 the Almshouses Charity was regulated by a Charity Commissioners' scheme, when the row of almshouses in Bedford Street together with 42 acres of land in Lidlington and Steppingley, was accepted by the Trustees from the Bedford Estate in satisfaction of the Estate's previous liabilities. The almshouses were converted into flatlets for retired parishioners in 1968 and renamed Staunton House. The last person to reside in an almshouse was Mrs Bowden. She was in her nineties when she died and could remember that, as a child, she used to walk from Pinfold with her mother, carrying a washing basket full of sandwiches and other goods to sell to the passengers of the old stage coaches.

The responsibility for the upkeep of roads and care of the poor was laid on the parish in the reign of Elizabeth I. Two Overseers of the Poor were nominated each year. The parishes of Aspley Guise, Battlesden, Chalgrave, Eversholt, Harlington, Hockliffe, Hulcote, Husborne Crawley, Milton Bryan, Potsgrove, Ridgmont, Salford, Tilsworth, Tingrith, Toddington and Woburn were combined to form a small Poor Law Union of which Woburn was head, and the new Union Workhouse covering some three acres was built in the area of Woburn known as White City or London End. It was built as a quadrangle and had an entrance hall 23' × 16' with receiving wards and the porter's room next door, a large dining room 53' × 16', five day rooms, a large laundry with drying, ironing and airing rooms, a carpenter' shop, a shoemaker's shop and a large bakehouse fitted with a five bushel oven. On the ground floor were wards for male and female vagrants and a fever hospital. Fourteen dormitories were on the first floor with store and staff rooms, committee and board rooms and a kitchen. The outbuildings consisted of barns, stables, four pigsties and sheds in which blocks of granite were broken up (for the making up of roads) by vagrants in return for a night's shelter and food. The minute book of the Guardians' meetings says: 'The advantage of a workhouse as an asylum for orphans and other children . . . is observable in their improved appearance and conduct . . . They daily receive instruction in their religious and moral duties, and are taught to read and write'. The girls had their hair cut short, wore long striped dresses and were only allowed out of the building to go to school. Women with illegitimate children were not accepted. In May 1836 the Master of the Workhouse was authorised 'to allow aged and infirm men 2oz. of bread in lieu of an ounce of cheese to be deducted, and 16oz. of suet pudding in lieu of 14oz. per day' and on 19 December 1836: 'Beef and plum pudding to be allowed on Christmas Day to all inmates of the workhouse, together with half a pint of ale for dinner, with the exception of the able bodied men only'.

The Woburn Union, however, did not work economically or efficiently. In 1898 the drainage, sanitation and water supply equipment was unsatisfactory and the estimate for repairs or replacement substantial. A local government inquiry was made and a meeting called for residents of Woburn and other villages in the Union but, although a majority opposed abolition, the Woburn Poor Law Union was dissolved on 29 September 1899. The site of the Union Workhouses was sold to the Duke of Bedford for £3,000 on 8 December 1899 and soon after that the buildings were demolished.

Woburn has produced few unworthy persons of note, but James Clare was one who received his final sentence through an incident in the workhouse. He had constantly made appearances in court for poaching but in 1831 he appeared, because he had threatened the mistress of Woburn Union Workhouse with a poker for not giving him more meat, pudding and potatoes. It was his last appearance, because he died in prison in 1834, his 78th year.

In 1850 the Woburn Gas Company Works was built on the north side of Leighton Street down what is now called Gas Lane. The contractor was Thomas Atkins, a gas engineer of Oxford. It was to be erected in three months for £1,900 and was paid for by the Estate. £100 was withheld for 6 months after the first night of lighting, to ensure that the work had been properly done, and the contractor provided a maintenance service for one year. Gas mains were laid from Woburn to the Abbey and Park Farm and lights were fitted. Gas lights were also fitted at the Market House (Town Hall) and Church.

In 1912 a water supply and sewerage system was installed for all the Duke's tenants, free of charge. This must have greatly improved conditions in the town since waste was either disposed of by pails into the garden or cleared periodically by sewage carts. 'Fresh' water was collected from wells or tanks.

The Duke also installed electric lighting for his tenants about 40 years ago, with a small increase in rent, and street lighting, which was paid for from the rates.

The welfare of the town also benefited from the medical care brought to them by the 'Flying Duchess'. Duchess Mary was much loved by the people of Woburn. She first developed what is now No 1 Leighton Street into a cottage hospital in 1898, fitting it out at her own expense and treating patients from Woburn itself free of charge. In 1903 she built another hospital on the outskirts of the town along the road to Leighton Buzzard. It was opened on 22 May and became known as the 'Woburn Clinic'. The Duchess worked there as a theatre sister and radiologist, being called 'Sister Mary' on the wards and, during the 1914-18 war, it was used for the treatment of wounded soldiers. At the outbreak of war in 1914 Her Grace turned the Abbey tennis court and riding school into Woburn Abbey War Hospital, equipping it with beds at her own expense and maintaining it throughout the six years of its existence. In 1917 the hospital became a special surgical unit for other ranks, receiving wounded men direct from the battlefields of France. By the end of the war 2,453 non-commissioned officers and men had passed through.

Woburn Clinic was taken over by the Bedfordshire Education Committee in 1967. It is now called 'Maryland' and is a residential college for adult education.

Woburn lost 41 of its young men in the 1914-18 war and on Sunday 5 September 1920 the war memorial was dedicated. During World War II more Woburn lives were lost and five more names were added to those already on the memorial.

ABOVE: The Town Hall built in 1830 by Edward Blore. On the left are the buildings that once stood on what is now the green. (MTTBE) BELOW: The Market Square facing north c1800. The old Market House, demolished in 1830, is the second building on the left. The George Inn (now the Bedford Arms) is on the right. From a painting by Paul Sandby. (MB)

ABOVE: The Market Square today. The Town Hall of 1830 by Edward Blore can clearly be seen now that the buildings on the corner of Leighton Street have gone. (JW) CENTRE: The old Pound in Timber (or Gas) Lane in 1936, after it had been repaired in 1932, (BM) though BELOW: repaired again in the 1950s, this is how it looks today. (A)

ABOVE: The old grammar school founded by Francis, 2nd Duke of Bedford, in 1582; it still stands today. (GIH) BELOW: Woburn schoolchildren earlier this century. (EA)

ABOVE: Woburn schoolboys. (JA) BELOW: Children of Woburn Infants School, 1908. Left to right — Back row: teacher Mrs Daisy Ames; Joe Stevens; E. Page; I. Sharpe; G. Goodman; J. Showler; F. Lewis; W. Rutland; H. Newbury; D. Showler; Middle Row: M. Short; E. White; W. Lewis; R. Palmer; E. Baker; W. Elkington; G. King; A. Champkin; Front row: J. Ames; A. Showler; E. Short; P. Palmer; L. Short; A. Champkin; W. Pepper. (JJ, whose Mother was the teacher).

LEFT: A sampler worked in Woburn by Elisabeth Skilton, in 1762.
(CS) RIGHT: The author's foster Mother, Polly Brown, making Bedfordshire
lace. (BT) BELOW: A pen and wash drawing of Woburn School by Brian Cairns
to commemorate the 400th Anniversary in 1982. (WS)

ABOVE: The Marquess of Tavistock, with the Headmistress, Miss J. Burleigh, and children of Woburn Lower School dressed in Tudor costume for the 400th Anniversary celebrations. (JRA) BELOW: The old fire engine house — now part of Woburn Lower School. (A)

ABOVE: The almshouses that originated from a bequest in the will of Sir Francis Staunton dated 1635. They have been converted into flatlets mainly for senior citizens and are now known as Staunton House. (JW) BELOW: An old range that was removed from the almshouses when they were converted into flatlets in 1968. On it was cast "THE WOBURN" GIBSON ANDREWS IRONMONGER WOBURN BEDS. (AB)

LEFT: Mrs Bowden, the last resident of the old almshouses before they were made into flatlets. She lived there until she died at the age of 93. (EPE) RIGHT: James Clare (1762-1834). He was sent to prison many times for poaching, but the last time was for threatening the Mistress of the Union Workhouse. (BCRO)

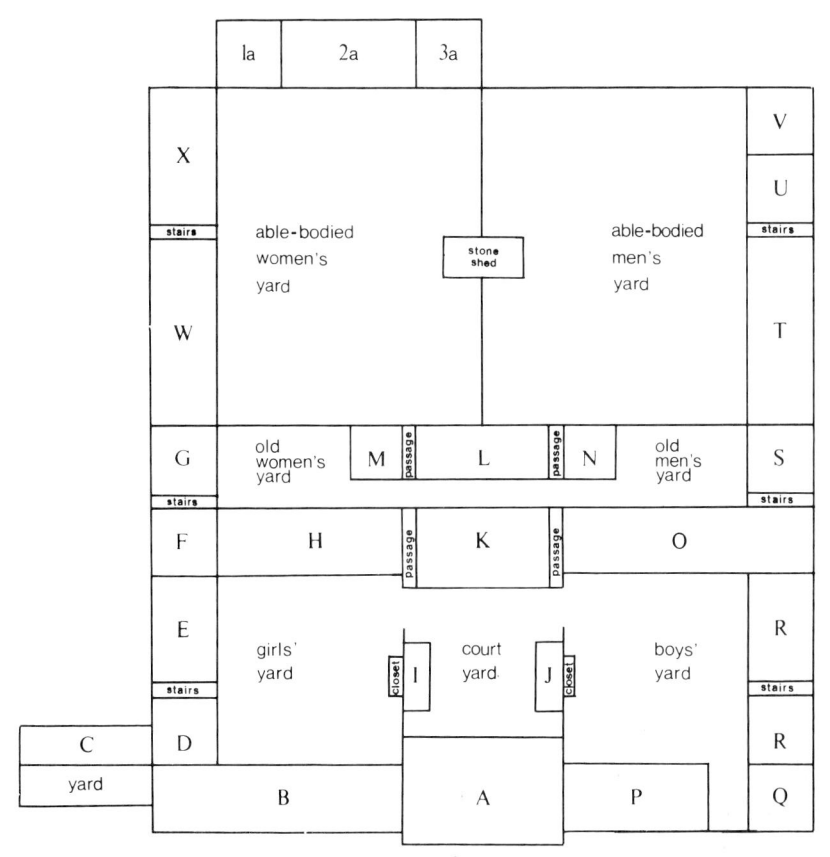

A plan of Woburn Union Workhouse based on one prepared for fire insurance with the Sun Insurance Co, 27 July 1867. The value of the property was assessed at £3,700. (A) Key to the rooms shown:

Ground Floor
A Waiting room, porter's room
B Offices
C Tramps' ward
D Girls' wash room
E Larder
F Old women's work room
G Old women's room
H Dining room
I Larder
J Scullery
K Kitchen
L Boys' day room
M Maids' and Mistresses' room
N Refractory room
O Bread room and bakehouse
P Coal and wood house
Q Tramps' ward
R Work rooms
S Old men's day room
T Kitchen
U Scullery
V Dining room
W Young women's day room
X Women's work room
1a Ironing room
2a Wash house
3a Drying room

First Floor
A Board room, receiving room
C Fever ward
D Bedrooms
E Storeroom
F Bedroom
G Bedroom
H Bedroom
K Mess Room
L Bedroom
O Bedroom
P Dead House
Q Bedroom
R Boys' bedrooms
S Bedroom
T Box room
V Bedroom

WOBURN, BEDFORDSHIRE.

TO INVESTORS, MANUFACTURERS, COMPANY PROMOTERS, AND OTHERS

Particulars and Conditions of Sale
OF A
HIGHLY VALUABLE
FREEHOLD PROPERTY
KNOWN AS
"THE UNION WORKHOUSE,"
WITH
Extensive Outbuildings and Gardens,
Situate in the Centre of the Town of Woburn,

THE WHOLE COMPRISING

3 ACRES
(MORE OR LESS;

TO BE SOLD BY AUCTION, BY

SWAFFIELD & SON

At the Bedford Arms Hotel, Woburn.

On FRIDAY, DECEMBER 8th, 1899,

At 4.30 for 5 o'clock in the Evening, in ONE LOT, by direction of the last ACTING GUARDIANS OF THE POOR OF THE WOBURN UNION (dissolved).

W. H. SMITH, Esq.,   MESSRS. SWAFFIELD & SON
Solicitor,   /
WOBURN.   AMPTHILL.

SMITH, PRINTER, AMPTHILL.

A poster advertising the sale of the Union Workhouse on 8 December 1899. (L-L)

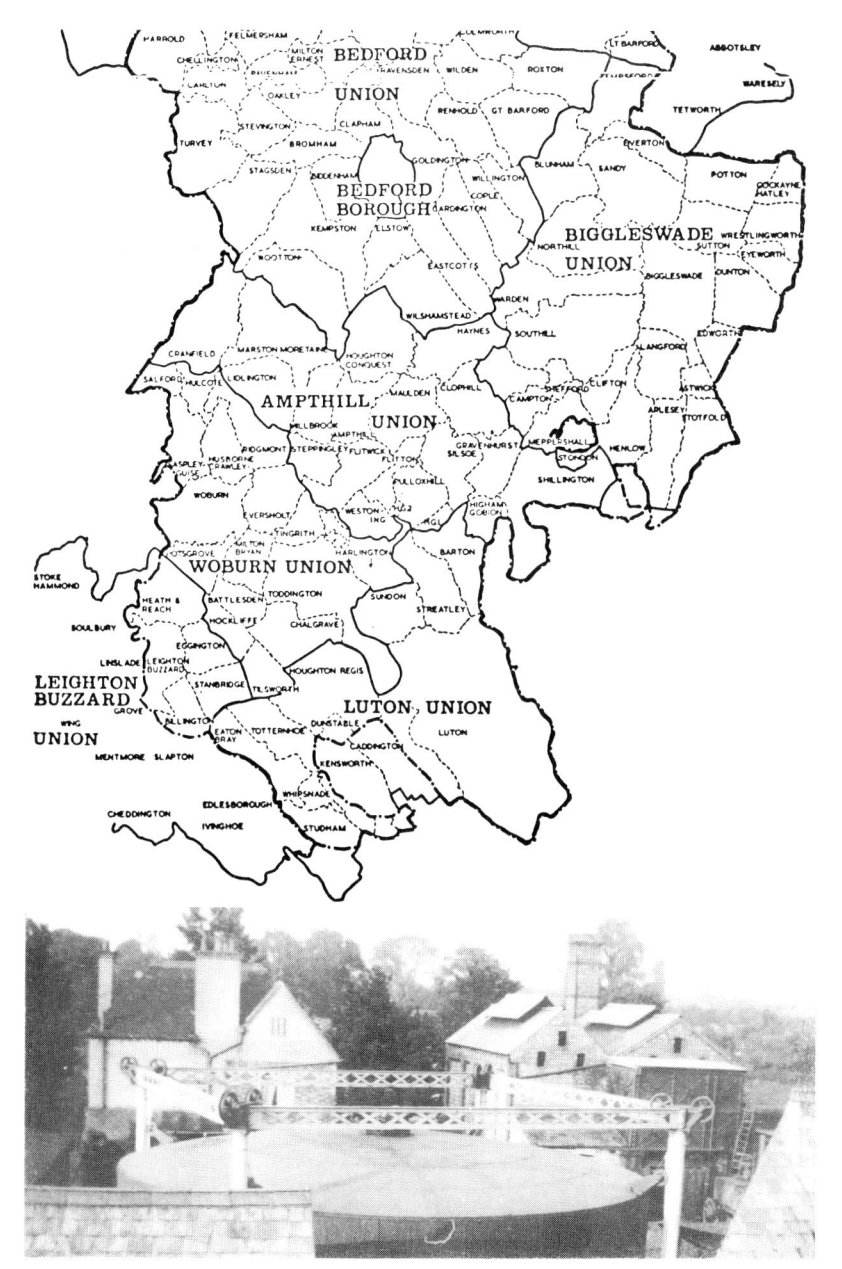

ABOVE: Bedfordshire Boundaries in 1834, showing the villages that comprised the Woburn Union. (BCRO) BELOW: Woburn Gasworks. The Gas Company was founded in 1850 and demolished in the 1950s. Charles G.A. Howard was the last manager. (GIH)

ABOVE: The 4.5 hp National gas engine that was used in the gasworks. In 1876 coke was 16s a ton. (GIH) BELOW: A scraperboard design of No 1 Leighton Street by Arthur E. Bayntun. Duchess Mary converted it into a cottage hospital. (AB)

ABOVE: Mary, Duchess of Bedford, known as the 'flying Duchess' and also 'Sister Mary' on the wards of the hospitals which she established. (MTTBE) BELOW: Maryland, built by Duchess Mary as a hospital in 1903. It is now a residential centre for adult education run by Bedfordshire Education Service. (JW)

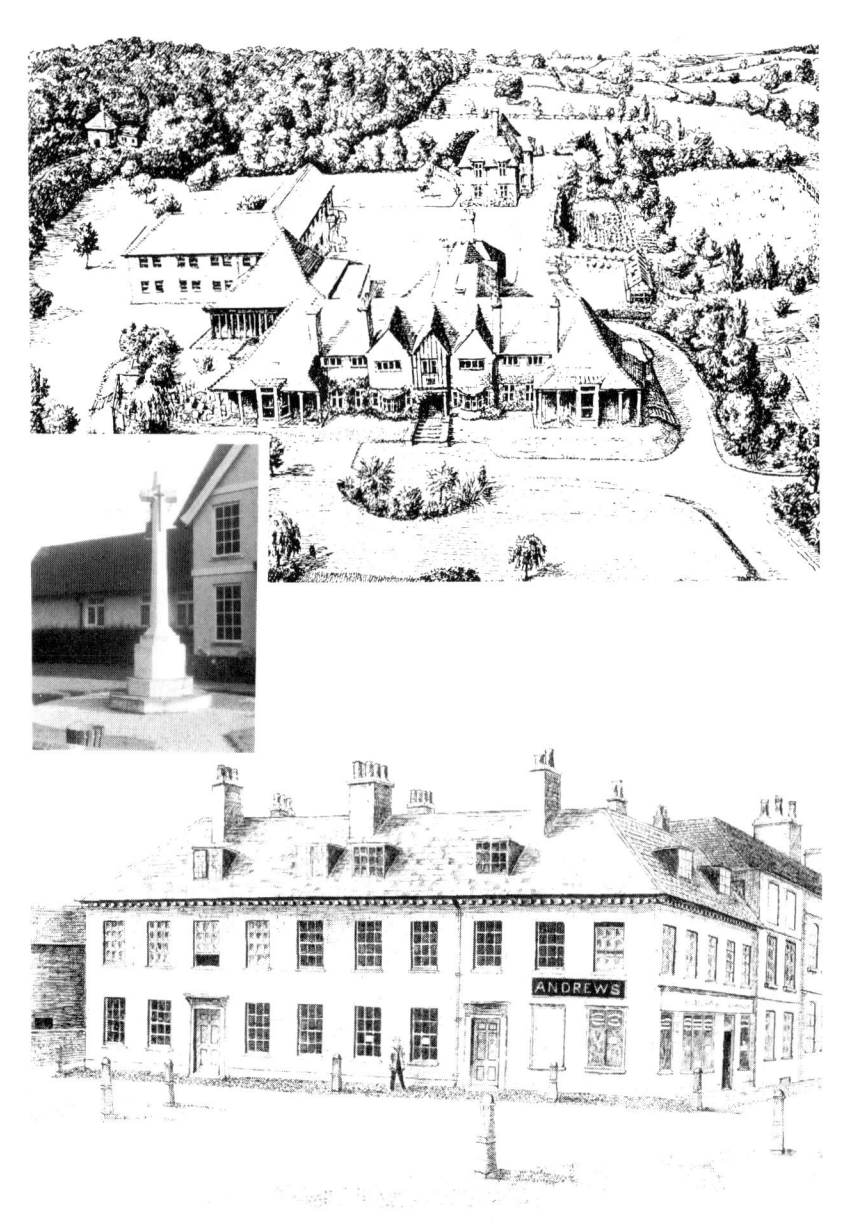

ABOVE: A plan view of Maryland drawn by Brian Cairns. (MC) BELOW: 'A piece of departed Woburn' (January 1912 by SAA); the buildings that used to be next to the Bedford Arms, now the war memorial. (A) INSET: Woburn War Memorial, unveiled and dedicated on 5 September 1920. (A)

The New Church

When the old church was pulled down in 1864, because it was supposedly too small, William, 8th Duke of Bedford, had the 'new', and present parish church built in Park Street. On entering the church there is a marble plaque set in the wall on the left near the tower with the inscription:

'In the years 1865-66-67-68, William, 8th Duke of Bedford built this church. OPERA ET CONSILIO HENRICI CLUTTON ARCHIT.'

The Act of Consecration stated that: 'The said new church be called, The Church of Saint Mary, Woburn, in substitution for the old church . . . and all the sittings therein (except those in the Chancel) to be free and unappropriated'.

The building is in the continental Gothic style of the 13th century, and although the first estimate was £10,246 3s, by the time the church was finished the cost had risen to £25,000.

The church consists of a chancel, nave of five bays, three aisles, vestry and a large crypt under the chancel. In 1868 a faculty was granted to the Dukes of Bedford, assigning them the crypt as a burial place for their family and successors for ever, exclusive of all others. However, at the time of writing members of the Russell family are still buried in the Bedford Chapel at Chenies Parish Church, and the crypt at Woburn is currently used for various church functions. According to the late Professor Richardson, authorities regard the church as one of the finest examples of Gothic revival in England. He commented that it is spacious and austere, the vaulted construction of the nave and aisle roof being unique. Records say that the church has accommodation for 650 people. In 1968 however, 670 packed into the church to hear the choir of King's College, Cambridge, but a more realistic number for most functions would be 500.

When the church was built in 1868 it had a tower and a square spire which together were 200 feet high. Twenty years later, in 1888, the structure was found to be unsafe, perhaps because of the vibration from the swinging of the 55cwt bell in the tower. On 6 October 1890 a parish meeting was called in the Town Hall. The spire was acknowledged to be dangerous in 1892, it was dismantled and the tower restored at a cost of £3,500. 1,000 scaffold poles and 670 scaffold boards were used, which were later sold off at auction to help defray the cost, together with some

4,760 bricks, 2,500 tiles and an enormous quantity of Portland and Bath stone. Of the three grotesques on the tower, the ones on the north-west and south-west corners were once described as those of the devil, and it was said, with some humour, that one peered down on the then churchwarden's house and the other at the vicarage.

Initially, the inside of the church was austere. The only woodwork in the chancel was the priest's desk and the altar rail with a large wooden cross about 10 feet high in a recess in the wall high above the altar. An embroidered panel was placed above the altar below the cross. This panel is still in position and in 1970 was netted by the Royal School of Needlework to preserve it. The pulpit was of stone and entrance to it was by stone steps with a wrought iron fence and gate leading from the corner of the church, under what is now the window of St Francis of Assisi. A small organ built by Thomas Robson was at the back of the church where the Lady Chapel now is. It was set in a gallery facing the entrance to the church. The choir also sat in this area. A font of Bath stone designed by Henry Clutton was placed at the back of the church.

In 1893 the Duchess Adeline bought a large carpet for the chancel, which is still in place, and drapes to hang on either side of the altar. The following year the stained glass windows, above and on either side of the altar, were given by her in memory of her husband Francis, 10th Duke of Bedford.

In 1902 the oak choir stalls and panelling were installed in the chancel together with the wrought iron railings. The stone pulpit was removed and replaced by the present one of oak with canopy, to the design of J.E. Kempe. This work cost £2,675 and was paid for by Herbrand, 11th Duke of Bedford. The priest's desk was moved from its place by the pulpit to its present position on the opposite side, and the desk that had been used from 1868-1902 was put in the Mortuary Chapel. To the right of the pulpit, as one faces the chancel, is a door known as the 'Duke's door'. It was put there after the old stone pulpit was taken down in 1902, so that the Duke could use it to enter and leave the church privately.

The Vestry Minutes record that also in 1902 new cupboards were fitted in the vestry, and discussions took place about draughts in the church (which are still present!). In 1903 the old bibles on the lectern and the prayer books on the priest's desk were considered too large, so the Duke bought smaller ones.

The magnificent reredos above the altar was presented in 1903 as well. It was designed by W.D. Caroe and the work was executed in Oberammergau; the subject is 'The adoration of the magi'. When the reredos was fitted, the drapes, which had been on either side of the altar, were removed as was the large cross above the altar. 1903 also saw the introduction of a cross and candlesticks on the altar, and these are still used today. Because of the threat of theft and vandalism they are only used during services; a set of turned wood, black and gold cross and candlesticks made by the author in 1981/82 are in position at other times.

In 1904 the Robson organ was replaced with the present instrument, a three manual built by Norman and Beard, which is reputed to be one of the finest village church organs in the country. It was placed in its present position at the north side of the nave near the chancel, instead of at the back of the church, in the organ loft designed by J.E. Kempe at a cost of £2,550.

Over the altar of the present Lady Chapel hangs the painting of *The Virgin and Child* by Carlo Maratti, originally part of the panel behind the altar in the old church. When the church was pulled down the painting was taken to the Abbey for safe-keeping. When Rev Charles Russell Dickinson was incumbent (1900-1913) he was walking round the Abbey with Herbrand, 11th Duke of Bedford one day and drew the Duke's attention to the painting and that it belonged to the church. As proof he produced a photograph showing it over the altar in the old church. It was returned and placed in the new church the following year. The old reredos was restored and placed in the Mortuary Chapel with a tapestry centre panel. Now there is a black and white print of the Virgin and Child in this panel and no one knows what happened to the tapestry.

Also used in the old church were the two bibles on the desk under the organ loft steps, dated 1737 and 1855. The oldest one was once lost, when the old church was pulled down, and no more was heard of it until 1914, when the then vicar of Woburn, Rev R.H. Moss, MA heard from Mrs G.H. Edmonson: '. . . to ask if you would like me to return the bible which belonged to Woburn church in 1737. I bought it at an old curiosity shop in Bedford in March 1903,[who]bought it from a Mr Puddaphett of Bedford who got the old Woburn Sexton to buy it at the sale of a Mrs Hall-Baker of Woburn . . . I shall be pleased to return it . . '.

In 1909 a new heating system was fitted at a cost of £450 and in 1915 purple chalice veil, burse and alms bags were purchased. An old red altar frontal was dyed purple also, to be used in Lent and Advent.

In the east wall of the south aisle is a stained glass window, installed in 1938 to the memory of Mary, Duchess of Bedford, the 'Flying Duchess'. The window depicts St Francis and no less than 58 birds — all that were to be found in the Park at that time.

In 1946 the present altar in the Lady Chapel was given by the then incumbent, Rev T.N. Gunner. It was originally the High Altar in the church of St Mary the Virgin, Tunstall.

1955 saw the old coke-fire boilers replaced with oil-fired ones at a cost of £832 and in 1956 Miss Madeleine Lovell, LRAM gave the Aumbry, with its carved and painted door and the Hobourn family presented the Litany desk in memory of their parents, Robert and Sarah Bell Hobourn.

The standard candlesticks in the Sanctuary were designed and carved from oak in 1957 by the author. The oak was grown on the Woburn Estate and was paid for by a local farmer, Mr D.O. Woodward.

For the centenary of the church in 1968 it was decided to improve the Lady Chapel. During that year new chairs were bought, made from

Austrian steamed beech. The Parochial Church Council thought it necessary to have matching altar rails and the author was asked to design and make them. The wood for this was purchased from the same firm that made the chairs and enough was left over for the author to also design and make the Credence table and a revolving Missal stand (unfortunately recently stolen) for the altar. The author also made the cross and candlesticks on the altar from Utile wood. The figure on the cross of Christ crucified was carved by a sister of the Community of St Clare, Freeland, Oxfordshire. New kneelers for the Lady Chapel were made by local ladies under the supervision of the author's wife, Frances Spavins. These included long kneelers for the altar rails as well as individual kneelers.

On the west wall near the Lady Chapel is a copy painted by B.J. Phillimore of the *Descent from the Cross* by Reubens. This was given to the church by Mrs Avis. The Tanqueray family gave the processional cross, 'In memory of Raymond Andrews and Baron Tanqueray, who were the first boys to lead this choir in procession, March 1901, and who died fighting on the Somme, July 1916'.

The wrought iron brackets that hold the banners of the Royal British Legion were made by the author from the wrought iron that was once by the side of the old stone pulpit steps. The gate at the bottom of the organ loft stairs was also part of the same ironwork and fitted at the same time to keep out vandals. The author also designed and made the portable hymn board at the request of Rev T. Wenham. Around the walls of the church are the eight commemorative armorial plates which originally hung in the old church.

Since 1732 the parishes of Battlesden and Pottesgrove have been a united benefice with Woburn. However, Pottesgrove church was declared redundant in 1971, no services are held there now and it is in the care of the Redundant Churches' Fund. For some years Eversholt and Milton Bryan have had no incumbent and have been linked with Ridgmont and Woburn respectively. However, when Rev Paul Miller came to Woburn in 1979 he was designated Priest-in-charge of Woburn, Eversholt, Milton Bryan, Battlesden and Pottesgrove but, by an order in Council effective 1 March 1982, he became Vicar of Woburn and Rector of Eversholt, Milton Bryan and Battlesden with Pottesgrove in a united benefice.

Not a great deal is known about the music of the old church. However, when it was pulled down in 1864 its 'Snetsler' organ was put into Eversholt church.

When the present church was built in 1868 an organ by Thomas Robson of London was positioned in a gallery at the back where the Lady Chapel now is. This instrument was used until the end of 1903 when it was dismantled, transported and re-erected by Norman and Beard in the Baptist Church at Foots Cray in Kent at a cost of £700.

In 1904 the present organ was installed. It is a fine three-manual instrument by Norman and Beard. It was built to the specifications of the then organist, William Steff-Langston, in consultation with the late

Herbert Norman. The motor power for the blower of this organ was at first a 7hp Crossley 'Otto' gas engine built in 1904 (unfortunately sold for scrap about 1963) which was used until 1952 when an electric motor was installed.

Organists at Woburn were: from 1868 (the Old Robson Organ): John Gilby senior; Jennie Gilby; John Gilby, and from 1904 (the Norman and Beard Organ): William Steff-Langston; Frederick Mason (afterwards organist at Hong Kong Cathedral); J. Charles Williams (formerly a sub-organist at Gloucester Cathedral); Claude Allen; John Henry String, ARCO; Cyril John Mitchell, Mus Bac, FRCO; Cyril Gell; Henry Marshall Palmer, ARCO; Albert Victor Chubb (for 23 years); Malcolm Stiff; Jack Humberstone and Roger Lander.

The old Abbey apparently had five bells, for the land revenue of 1556 records: 'The Lorde Wyllyams for V bellys of the late Monasterye of Woborne solde by hym by the reporte of W. Smythe, Surveyor'.

An old inventory of 1651 in the Churchwardens' chest said that the old church possessed five bells in 1556. There were three broken bells with clappers, one whole bell, an iron clock with a bell 'proper to it' and also a Saint's bell that hung in an open cupola on top of the tower. This was moved to the old Town Hall, and taken to Park Farm during restoration on the Town Hall and then stolen. The bells were housed in the tower at the side of the old church.

In 1663 four bells were recast at a cost of £120 of which £90 was given by the Earl of Bedford; a new 5th was added in 1724 or it may have been that the clock bell was utilised. In 1829, two of the bells being broken and the others being out of tune, they were taken down and sent to the Whitechapel foundry, where a larger ring of six in the key of G flat was cast from them and hung in time for the proclamation of William IV. The estimated cost was £384, raised by public subscription and a donation of £100 from the Duke of Bedford. The weights of these bells with their inscriptions were:

	cwt	qr	lbs	
Treble	5	2	7	T. Mears of London Fecit 1829
2nd	6	0	2	T. Mears of London Fecit 1829
3rd	6	1	4	T. Mears of London Fecit 1829
4th	7	1	17	His Grace John 5th Duke of Bedford
5th	9	3	26	The Rev Thomas Roy
6th	12	3	19	Joseph Tween / William Freeman Churchwardens 1829

(There is an error in the inscription for it was the 6th Duke of Beford not the 5th).

For many years a 'curfew' bell was rung at 4 am and again at 8 pm. An entry in the Vestry Minutes of 1750 says 'Mr Seer payed £2 6s 9d per annum'. The practice was kept up at least until 1832.

In 1877, mainly through the efforts of a ringer called Charles Herbert, two new trebles were added to the ring of six to make 'one of the nicest little peals in the neatest little steeple'. The bells were fitted with silencers invented by a Mr Seage of Exeter and were known as 'Seage's Tell Tales'. The bells could be rung for any length of time without disturbing the townspeople. For the opening, Grandsire and Stedman Triples, Kent Treble Bob Major and Superlative Surprise Major ('that most intricate and beautiful specimen of art and rarely attempted by any but the elite of the ringing fraternity') were rung.

About this time Woburn had a keen band who regularly practised change ringing. They had subscribed for and bought a set of twelve handbells and a library of books on campanology. The handbells cost £8. A set of 16 rules of behaviour was drawn up on 21 November 1867. The first one reads: 'We resolve to be a respectable body of men as well as good ringers and to give no occasion to any person to speak against us or bring disgrace on the church. We will not take into our Company any person of low character, for the belfry is part of the church and the ringers should bear a good character. Notice of any special ringing shall be given by the foreman, any ringer who shall not attend shall forfeit sixpence'. Any ringer who was late for service ringing by 15 minutes had to pay twopence and anyone leaving the belfry before the bells were pulled down was fined a penny. There were separate rules for the handbells, although the tower bell ringers were also the handbell ringers. There was also a list of probationary ringers (learners) who were not liable for fines but could receive a share of any profits when acting as regular ringers.

When the new church was completed in 1868 a single bell weighing 55cwt was hung in the tower. It had a diameter of 63 inches and was cast by Mears and Stainbank, London in 1867. It was rung up by three men half an hour before the service began, then there was a pause for 10 minutes, after which it was rung again for 10 minutes and then the bell was lowered. The ringers were paid 3s each Sunday by the Duke.

In 1910, again mainly because of the efforts of Charles Herbert, the Duke of Bedford was persuaded to install a peal of eight bells in the new church. They were cast from the metal of seven bells from the old church tower (leaving one for the clock chime) together with the metal of the large bell in a new church tower. They are in the key of D and their weights are:

	cwt	qr	lbs		cwt	qr	lbs
Treble	6	2	13	5th	11	2	18
2nd	7	0	0	6th	12	3	2
3rd	8	0	19	7th	17	1	13
4th	9	1	27	Tenor	24	1	16

The inscription on the tenor reads:

'This peal, recast from 7 bells in the old tower and from the large bell formerly hanging in this tower, was presented to the church of St Mary, Woburn by Herbrand XI Duke of Bedford K.G., on Christmas Day

A.D. 1910. C.R. Dickinson MA., Vicar, C.P. Hall, W.T. Hulatt, Churchwardens.'

Two medallions were cast from the metal of the old bells; one was presented to the vicar, Revd C.R. Dickinson and the other to W.J. Hulatt, one of the Churchwardens.

The handbells from the old church are believed to have been sold. There is a set in a chest marked 'Woburn Company of Change Ringers 21st Nov. 1867' in Luton Museum, but some people dispute their authenticity. In 1955 a new set of twelve handbells was presented to the church by the widow of William Ernest Herbert, son of Charles Herbert. The handbells were dedicatd by Rev T.N. Gunner in November 1955. These bells have been added to over the years and for many years the author had a young band of handbell ringers who played tunes at many functions. The bells are now used by the Girl Guides under the direction of the author's wife, Frances Spavins.

Many boards recording peals rung on both old and new church bells hang in the present church's belfry. The most recent peal was one of London Surprise Major rung on 30 January 1983 in memory of the author of this book.

For over 20 years the author was Tower Captain at Woburn and taught many a Woburn youth to ring on the silenced clock bell in the old church tower. The tradition of 'ringing in the new year' was kept at midnight on New Year's Eve, but general enthusiasm waned and in recent years the tradition was no longer practised. It was always a struggle to maintain a band of ringers for Sunday service ringing and today the bells remain silent except for one bell rung before services and the occasional ringing by visiting bands.

Woburn ringers have contributed much to the Bedfordshire Association of Church Bell Ringers inasmuch as Charles Herbert was mainly responsible for its founding. He was the first secretary and was later a vice-president. Sidney Avis designed the Association's membership certificate and the author designed and introduced the Association's badge as well as being secretary of the Luton District for 20 years.

Charles Herbert was born in Sudbury, Suffolk (in 1844) and began change-ringing in 1863. He was a lawyer's clerk and came to Woburn in 1865 when he was 21. Although there had been bands of change-ringers previously in the county, when he came to Bedfordshire there were none, but because of his great efforts in this field he became known as the 'Father of change-ringing in Bedfordshire'.

In 1865, when he arrived in Woburn, the Mortuary Chapel and the new church were being built, but ringing continued on the six bells in the old church tower. In 1877 Charles persuaded the Duke to add two more bells, making a ring of eight. In 1882 the Woburn Company rang their first 720 of Plain Bob Minor, which was the first in the county for 200 years, and that same year Charles founded the Bedfordshire

Association of Church Bell Ringers, which is still active today, becoming its first secretary. He was fond of string music and kept open house for musicians as well as bell ringers. He also used to enjoy taking the Woburn Company to ring handbells around the lantern on top of the old church tower. As a lawyer's clerk he was skilled in writing copperplate and won a prize in 1875 for an 'illuminated Anglican Missal' as well as designing peal-boards for many belfries. In 1910, his 66th year, he was instrumental in having the bells recast and moved from the old church tower to the new church. He had two sons, Cyril and Ernest, both of whom became ringers, and he died on 12 September 1923, nearly 80 years of age.

Douglas Harris was one of Charles Herbert's original Woburn Company. He was born in Nantwich, Cheshire, in 1875 and moved to Woburn when he was 17 to work in the estate office of the Duke of Bedford in Woburn Park, from which he retired 47 years later as head accountant. He was founder and secretary of the local football, tennis and bowls clubs, in all of which he took part as a player.

Charles Herbert taught him to ring in 1895 and he joined the Bedfordshire Association the same year. His first peal was on the eight bells in the old church in 1897. His first on handbells, Plain Bob Royal, took place in 1902 at the house of Mr Herbert. He rang about 50 peals in all, about half of which were in hand. He was vice-president and trustee of the Bedfordshire Association, tower captain, Vicar's warden, sidesman, in the choir and on the PCC. He always referred to the bells of the present church as 'my bells'.

In 1931 he went on a ringers' pilgrimage to Belgium and rang a unique course of Grandsire Triples in hand with 1-2, 3-4 in France and 5-6, 7-8 in Belgium on the border.

When he was 82 he was knocked down by a car and sustained a dislocated shoulder, which put him out of action for a time, but the tail end of the 4th (his favourite bell) was lengthened and he was soon ringing again. He continued to do so until he was unable to climb the steps to the belfry, but was able to ring London in hand to celebrate his 90th birthday. He was meticulous in everything he did and kept a day-to-day diary right up to the end of his life at the age of 92.

We know of three parsonages in which the incumbents of Woburn have lived since the middle of the 18th century. The first of these is known as the Old Parsonage and stands within the gates of the old churchyard in the High Street. It is a Georgian building built in 1756 and designed by Sir William Chambers. It was the residence of the priests of Woburn until 1873; the last one to have lived there is believed to have been Rev Samuel Francis Cumberlege. Since then it has been used for the Sunday School; for the distribution of Charity Bread; to house refugees during the 1914-18 war and as a Working Men's Club. After this it fell into disrepair but has been restored by Mr and Mrs Sykes and is now both an antique shop and their home.

In 1873 the large house on the north-east corner of the Woburn-Ampthill turning became the next vicarage. This was described as a large villa and was built in 1864 to the designs of Edward Blore. The house was previously occupied by a local grocer and corn merchant. Rev T.N. Gunner was the last priest to live there and also the first to live in the present vicarage which is in Park Street. It was built in 1960 and was first occupied in December of that year.

Woburn parish church c1870. The tower and spire were 200 feet high and found to be unsafe in 1890. (L-L)

ABOVE: Woburn parish church after 1892 when the removal of the spire was completed, (CJR/SR) and BELOW: today. (JW)

ABOVE: The crypt at the time of an exhibition which was held there during a flower festival. (JW) BELOW: Inside Woburn parish church c1894. The chancel was austere and a large cross hung above the embroidered panel behind the altar. The drapes on either side of the altar were given in 1893 by Duchess Adeline, who also gave the stained glass window in memory of her husband in 1894. On the right is the old stone pulpit with its iron railings and gate. (JW/V)

ABOVE: Looking towards the altar in the present parish church at the time of a Flower Festival in 1974. The stained glass windows, reredos and embroidered panel can be seen at the east end with the oak panelling in the chancel added in 1902. On the left is part of the organ loft and on the right the oak pulpit and canopy.
(JW/V) BELOW: The two old Bibles belonging to the church (JW/V)

The main altar showing the reredos, carved in Oberammergau, above the original embroidered panel which was renetted by the Royal School of Needlework. The jewelled altar frontal was remounted by Frances Spavins, the author's wife. On the altar are the brass cross and candlesticks. (JW)

TO THE MEMORY OF
BRYDEN GLENDINING F.R.C.S.
SURGEON TO THE WOBURN ABBEY WAR HOSPITAL
FROM 1914 TO THE END OF THE WAR AND
SUBSEQUENTLY SURGEON TO THE WOBURN HOSPITAL.
BORN MARCH 29TH 1880 DIED MAY 19TH 1927.
"MADE WEAK BY TIME AND FATE, BUT STRONG IN WILL
TO STRIVE, TO SEEK, TO FIND, AND NOT TO YIELD."

ABOVE: The organ loft. This photograph featured on the front of an appeal leaflet for the restoration of the organ in 1974. (JW) BELOW: The memorial plaque to Bryden Glendining under the St Francis window. (JW/V)

LEFT: The Saint Francis window given in memory of Mary, Duchess of Bedford, 1865-1937. (JW/V) RIGHT: One of the two oak candlesticks made by the author. (JW/V)

LEFT: The processional cross. (JW/V) RIGHT: The carved door of the aumbry given by Miss M. Lovell. (JW/V) BELOW: The wrought iron gate at the bottom of the organ loft stops. It was once part of the ironwork on the steps leading to the old stone pulpit. (JW/V)

ABOVE: The Lady Chapel, site of the old organ gallery. The altar rails, cross, candlesticks, credence table and folding missal stand (recently stolen) were made by the author to match the chairs, for the church's centenary in 1968. (JW/V)
BELOW: A view inside the new church, decorated for a Harvest Festival in the late 1890s. (A)

LEFT: The copy of a painting by Rubens executed by B.J. Phillimore. (JW/V)
RIGHT: An experimental window of 'Grisaille' glass under the organ loft. (JW/V)
BELOW: John Gilby c1900. He was a draper in Woburn and was the last organist to play the old Robson organ. (A)

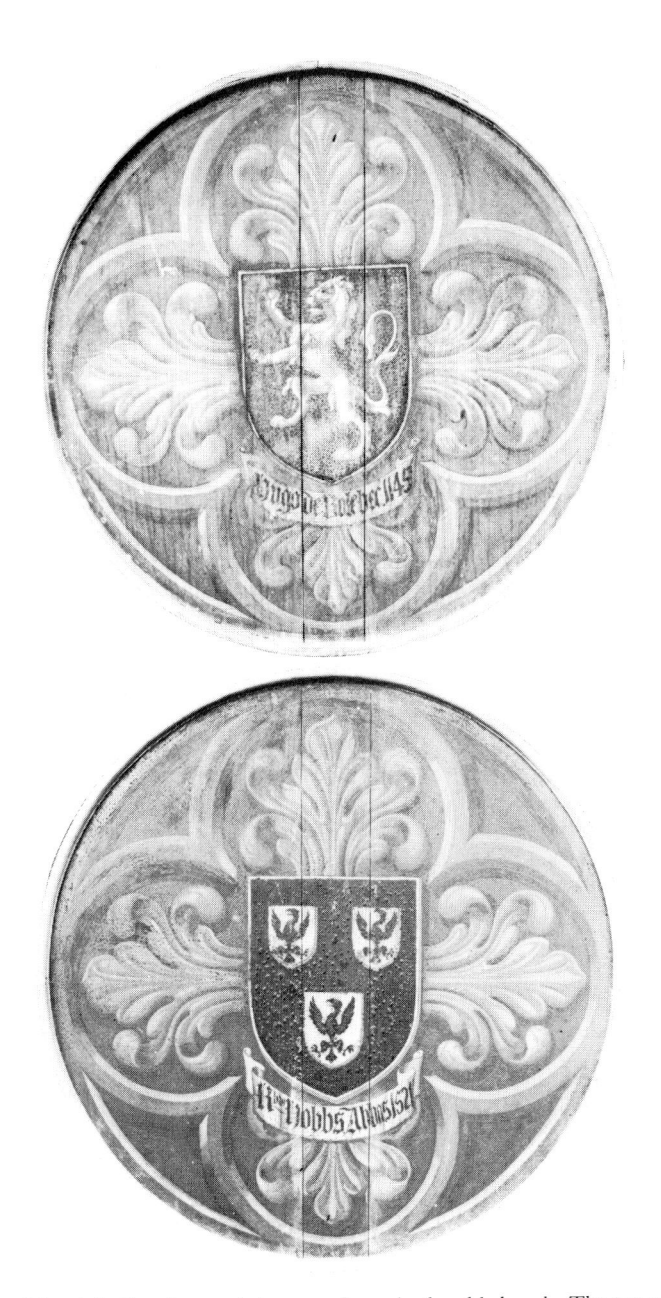

Two of the eight 'hatchments' that once hung in the old church. The top one is to 'Hugo de Bolbec', founder of the Abbey of St Mary at Woburn in 1145, and the lower one is to Robert Hobbs, who became the last abbot in 1529 and was hanged in 1538. (The date on it is 1521). (JW/V)

Augmentation of Woburn Bells.

THE Belfry of the old Tower is now complete with a peal of eight Bells, two additional ones, supplied by Messrs. Mears & Stainbank of London, having been recently added, and the old Bells and the Belfry thoroughly renovated, through the liberality of His Grace the Duke of Bedford.

The opening of the Bells will take place on MONDAY, THE 16TH APRIL inst., when Selections of Change-ringing will be performed by eminent Campanists.

> "If aught there be upon this rude bad earth
> Which Angels from their happy spheres above
> Could lean and listen to,
> It were those peaceful sounds."

Woburn, April 5th, **1877**.

ABOVE: The announcement of the opening of the augmented ring of bells in the old church, April 1877. (CJR/SR) OPPOSITE ABOVE: The Woburn ringers who rang the bells of Woburn's old and new churches at the end of the 19th century and beginning of the 20th century. They are, left to right — Back row: Cyril Herbert, H.D. Harris, Ernest Herbert, W.E. Turney; Front row: Charles Herbert, Sidney Avis, William Chibnall, Alfred Morrison. (A) CENTRE: The bells of the old church lying at the foot of the old church tower having been taken down to be recast as the present ring. (A) BELOW: The new bells being placed in the present parish church in 1910. (A)

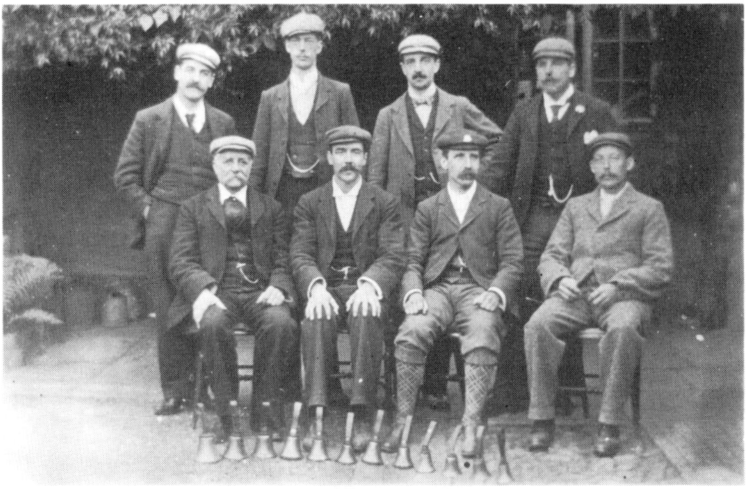

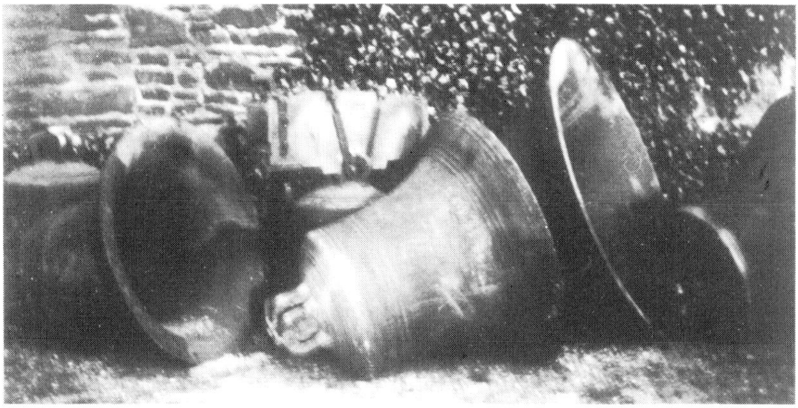

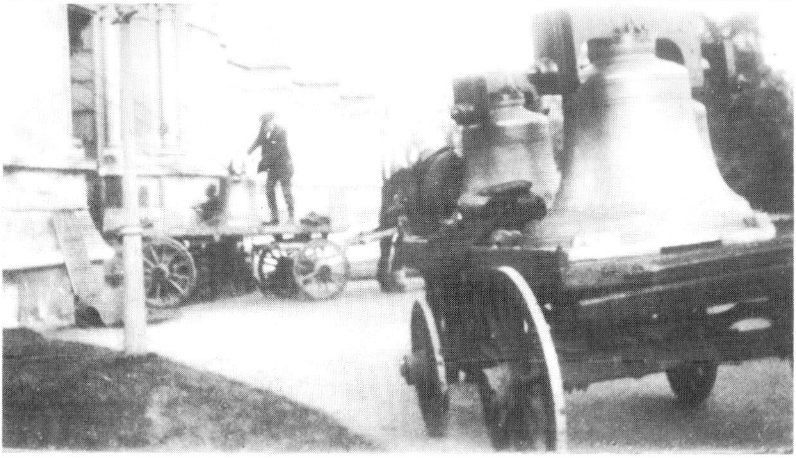

WOBURN.

THE EIGHT BELLS IN THIS TOWER were cast in December 1910, from the metal of the large bell which formerly hung here, together with seven of the bells out of the old tower, & erected by MEARS & STAINBANK OF LONDON. E.

	cwt	qrs	lbs	note
Tenor	24	1	16	D
7th	17	2	13	E
6th	12	3	2	F#
5th	11	2	18	G
4th	9	1	27	A
3rd	8	0	19	B
2nd	7	0	0	C#
Treble	6	2	13	D
TOTAL	97	2	24	

Inscription on Tenor

This peal, re-cast from seven bells in the old tower, and from the large bell formerly hanging in this tower, was presented to the Church of St Mary Woburn by HERBRAND XI Duke of Bedford, K.G. on Christmas Day. A.D. 1910.

C. R. Dickinson, M.A. Vicar.
C. P. Hall
W. T. Hulatt } Churchwardens.

The board in the belfry giving the weights and key of the present ring of eight in the new church. (JW/V)

It is proposed to establish in Woburn a Company of Bell Ringers who will bind themselves to be of good Character and live as worthy members of the Church. A Peal of Handbells will be required before any practice can be made on the Church Bells. The cost of this peal is estimated at from £5 to £8. Efficient instruction has been provided and there is every hope that much good may be done by the establishment of a respectable and reverent body of Ringers.

Your assistance and goodwill is most respectfully and earnestly solicited.

Name	Donation
W. D.	10
Wm Frederick Green	10
	10
	10
John Green	10
	10
John Thos Green	10
	2 6
J Sergeant	5 0
W. C.	2 6
	2 6
W. W.	10 —
Richard Shepherd	2 —
John Flinn	5
E T Tanqueray	1 0
A Friend AB	1 —
E Smith	1
	10
E.A. Hamer	10 —
	10
	10 0

The subscription list to purchase a set of handbells for the Company of Bell Ringers in Woburn, 1867. (A)

The membership certificate of the Bedfordshire Association of Change Ringers which was designed by Sidney Avis. The towers pictured are those of Woburn, Leighton Buzzard, Dunstable, and St Paul's Bedford. (JW/V)

4th June 1982
A QUARTER PEAL OF 1259 GRANDSIRE TRIPLES

1. Malcolm Melville
2. ~~Barbara Nichols~~
3. Charlotte H. Smith
4. James H. Edwards
5. Anthony H. Smith
6. Nigel Thacker
7. Keith Lewin
8. J E Jeffries

Conducted by Anthony H. Smith.

A thanksgiving for the life and work of Kenneth G. Spavins.

ABOVE: Signatures of those ringers who took part in a quarter peal, rung as a thanksgiving for the life and work of the author after the funeral on 4 June 1982. (JW/V) LEFT: Charles Herbert (1844-1923), who reintroduced change ringing to Bedfordshire, was a founder member of the Bedfordshire Association of Change Ringers and was its first secretary. He was also a keen musician. (JW/V) RIGHT: The badge of the Bedfordshire Association of Change Ringers, designed by the author. (JW/V) BELOW: The first quarter peal rung by the Woburn Company. It originally hung in the old church tower but is now in the belfry of the new church. (JW/V)

ABOVE: The Bedfordshire Association of Change Ringers at Easter 1900. (JW/V)
BELOW: H.D. Harris (1875-1967), the last of the old band of Woburn ringers, ringing the 4th, his favourite bell, in the belfry of the present parish church. Behind him can be seen part of one of the charity boards on the belfry walls. (BT)

ABOVE: The old parsonage and the gates that lead into the old churchyard, mortuary chapel and old church tower. (CS) BELOW: The old Vicarage built in 1864 to the designs of Edward Blore, architect to Queen Victoria and William IV. It is now a private residence. (SA)

LEFT: The Congregational chapel, built in 1804. It was sold in 1953 and is now a private residence. For a time it was the home and studio of the artist Derek Greaves. (JW) RIGHT: The Methodist chapel built in 1860. It was sold in 1963 and is now used by a furniture manufacturer. (JW) BELOW: No 8 Leighton Street, once a school for the sons of Quakers. (JW)

The Dissenters

Besides the Anglican church, Woburn has also had Congregational, Methodist and Baptist churches as well as a meeting of Quakers and a Quaker school.

The Congregational, or Independent community was in Woburn by 1789, when a house in West Street was used for meetings under the leadership of the surgeon, Robert Carey. In 1804 a Chapel was built in London End. The Chapel was enlarged several times and finally in 1899. Rev Samuel Greathead of Woburn Independents was influential in a wider field of mission work. In 1795 he was a founder of the inter-denominational London Missionary Society and he also put forward the idea of Baptists, Independents, Methodists and Moravians working together for mission work in the villages. He organised a meeting of ministers to discuss the proposal and in 1797 the Bedfordshire Union of Christians was formed, althought it was predominantly Baptist and Independent.

However, numbers eventually declined and the last service was held on 23 July 1944 with Rev Patrick Figgis as preacher. 1951 saw the beginning of a sale of contents and in June 1953 the building was sold. Until recently it was the home and studio of an artist and his wife.

Both Hockliffe and Newport Pagnell are mentioned in John Wesley's diary and it is possible that he passed through Woburn, although there is no record. In 1815 Woburn Methodists were attached to the Leighton Buzzard Circuit, meeting at one time in some cottages in Cobbs Row, and then transferring to the Wolverton Circuit in 1856/57. The membership was only 17 then, but in October 1860 the foundation stone of a church was laid in Leighton Street, at its junction with London End. The congregation continued to increase such that in 1886 a schoolroom was built for the growing Sunday School. In 1907 a new organ was bought to replace the harmonium, the organist of the time being Mr Steff Langston, before he became organist at the new Parish Church of St Mary in 1904. During the 20th century the congregation began to decline, although for a time it was augmented by the WRNS stationed at the Abbey and Woburn Clinic (Maryland) during the war and by members of the Congregational community after the closure of their own church. The Methodist church survived to celebrate its centenary in 1960 and at that time looked forward to continued worship in the building but it too was sold in October 1963 and is now used by a furniture manufacturer.

Woburn Baptists are mentioned in a Ridgmont Baptists' book of 1801 and as a strict Calvinistic Chapel in 1881. A building in Woburn was first registered for use as a chapel in 1835 and a purpose-built chapel was erected in 1842. All sittings were free and the congregations reached about 120 people in the morning and 140 in the afternoon. Thomas Goodwin was minister for a time; he moved from Pewsey to Woburn and first preached here in April 1844. He had a salary of 30s a week. However, as with many other things, attendance obviously declined, because well before the end of the 19th century the Baptist community seems to have disappeared.

There was a Quaker presence in Woburn at a fairly early date for, by the year 1655, Friends of the Woburn area were meeting at the home of Thomas Scott. Because of the political climate prevailing during the Commonwealth and after the Restoration, they were subject to harassment. A constable raided one of their meetings and made some arrests. In another incident Sarah Baker of Woburn was imprisoned for giving Christian exhortation 'in the public place of worship'. By 1670 the Woburn group was meeting in the house of William Albright, together with Friends of the area from Aspley Guise, Wavendon, Bow Brickhill and Little Brickhill. A local barber informed on them and goods from Albright's house were taken as payment of fines. Meetings continued with further seizures of goods until there was nothing suitable left and Albright was committed to prison. However, in 1672 a meeting house was bought at Woburn Sands (Hogsty End) and Friends from Woburn went there. But this did not prevent trouble for, in 1675, Buckinghamshire magistrate Thomas Hacket passed information about the Woburn members at Hogsty End to his Bedfordshire colleague St John Chernock. By 1822 the Woburn group of Friends had apparently combined with the Leighton group and met at the Leighton meeting house.

The Wiffen family were notable Quakers of Woburn. In the late 18th century Elizabeth Pattison married John Wiffen, a prosperous local ironmonger. John had a great love of poetry and literature and at least two of his six children inherited his interest. The eldest, Jeremiah Holmes Wiffen, was born on 30 December 1792 and his brother Benjamin Baron Wiffen on 28 October 1794. Jeremiah began his education at a private school in Woburn and after a short time at schools in Ampthill and Hitchin. He went to a Quaker school at Ackworth in Yorkshire at the age of ten. He developed an ability in etching and wood-engraving as well as poetry and at the age of fourteen left school to be apprenticed to a schoolmaster at Epping, Essex — a position he did not enjoy. During his teens some of his writings were published and at nineteen he returned to Woburn and opened his own school for the sons of Quakers at No 8 Leighton Street. He continued to write and study, becoming skilled in Latin, Greek, Hebrew, French, Italian, Spanish and Welsh. He also enjoyed mathematics, music and drawing. In 1821 he was appointed librarian at Woburn Abbey to the Duke of Bedford and in 1825 began *The Historical Memoirs of the House of Russell* which took him eight years. He married in 1828 and had three daughters, one of whom wrote his biography. He wrote and published all his life and died in 1836, being buried in the Friend's burial ground at Woburn Sands.

Benjamin joined Jeremiah at Ackworth in 1803 and spent five years there before returning to Woburn to help his mother carry on the family business after his father's early death. Benjamin was a reserved man, but one of high ideals. His poetic inclinations were subdued by a sense of duty. He was Overseer for Aspley Guise from 1849-1854. In his midforties he became physically weak, and retired with his mother and sisters to a cottage near Mount Pleasant in Aspley Guise, which gave opportunity for his literary interests and research to flourish. He never married and latterly lived a secluded life; he died at the age of 72 in 1867 and was buried near his brother.

A line drawing of Jeremiah Holmes Wiffen. (BM)

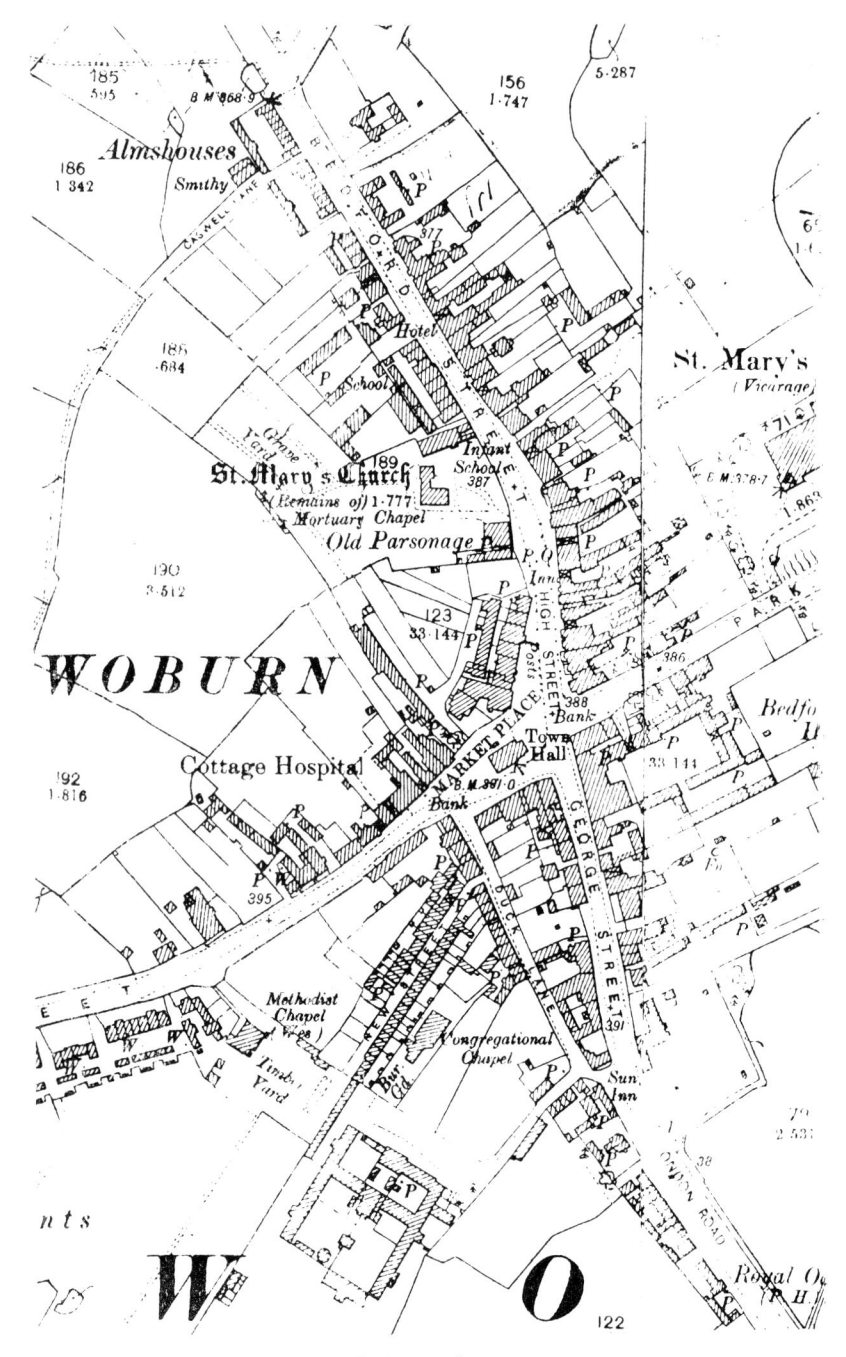

1901 Ordnance Survey map.

Woburn's Wheels

The 18th century was a time of increasing prosperity for Woburn. The market and fairs were well patronised, bringing people from afar into the town, benefiting local tradesmen. With this increase in prosperity came an increase in traffic which included coaches, carts and cattle as well as people. Until then most roads were simply grass lanes, which quickly became miry and rutted. Their upkeep was minimal. In the Middle Ages the lord of each manor had attended to this and public-spirited people had left money in their wills. In Woburn the Abbot would have supervised this work. However, during the 16th century the parish became a unit of civil and administrative authority and, in 1555, the Act for Mending of Highways made each parish responsible for the care of roads within its boundaries. Clearly no small parish could afford to maintain busy roads and a solution was sought in the turnpike, whereby a stretch of road was taken over by a group of gentlemen through an act of parliament. They provided capital and travellers paid to cover costs and interest.

The Hockliffe to Woburn road was the first to be turnpiked in Bedfordshire, in 1706, and was a section of the London to Northampton road after turning off the Watling Street. The Hockliffe to Woburn Act of 1706 explained that there was a substantial causeway in a lane at Hockliffe that was only suitable for horse and cattle, but that the rest of the lane to Woburn was broad but foundrous, and if it were to be made into a good carriage-road it would then be the best route to Northampton, Chester and the North. However the Watling Street was also turnpiked later in 1706 (it being 'very ruinous' and 'almost unpassable' until then) so probably it became the usual route to Chester after that.

The Woburn Tollhouse was one mile south of Woburn, about 100 yards north of the turning to Potsgrove. It stood on the east side, between the road and the park wall, just south of Shotters Cottage. We do not know what the road looked like but we can picture the traffic using it from the list of tolls set out in the Act:

'for every Stage Coach or Hackney Coach, One Shilling; for every other Coach, Calash, Chaise or other Chariot. One Shilling; For every Waggon, Wain or Cart Loaded with Wheat, Barley or any other Grain, Six Pence; For every other Waggon, One Shilling; And for every other Cart, Eight Pence; and for every Drove of Oxen or Neat Cattle, consisting of Seven or more in Number, Four Pence; and for every Drove of Sheep or Lambs, consisting of Forty or more in Number, Three Pence; And for every Drove of Hogs, consisting of Thirty or more in Number, Three Pence; and for every Gang of Pack-Horses, consisting of Seven or more (other than Horses Loaden with Wheat, Barley or any other Grain) Three Pence; and that from and after the Passing of the Act, all and every Person and Persons who shall at any time Travel in and through the Lane or Highway aforesaid shall and are hereby required to Pay Toll after the Rates aforesaid . . .'

Not everyone had to pay. Exemption was given to the clergy on official duty, the military, royal mail, agricultural horses and implements, vehicles carrying vagrants, those involved in road repair and those travelling to and from work, divine worship or parliamentary elections. However, a double toll was imposed on Sundays to discourage travel on the sabbath. Restrictions were also imposed on the size of wheels and over loading to avoid excessive damage to the road surface.

The Woburn-Hockliffe turnpike lasted from 1706-1877. In 1728 the road from Woburn to Tickford Bridge at Newport Pagell was added to the trustees' care and turnpiked, lasting until 1877 too. The inhabitants of Battlesden were also exempt from paying tolls in 1728. A weighing machine was erected at the Woburn Tollhouse, which was the subject of a special clause in the Renewal Act of 1780 for dealing with waggons which avoided it by using Sheep Lane to pass from Woburn to the Watling Street. A new road was made with a more easterly curve between Hockliffe and the first turning to Milton Bryan after 1821. Both routes are shown on the Ordnance Survey map of 1835 but the old route was disused after that.

The Woburn to Ampthill road was turnpiked between 1777 and 1872 near Flying Horse Farm (midway between Ampthill and Woburn) although the road did not come to Woburn until 1796. Originally it went from Ridgmont to Red Lodges (the north entrance to Woburn Park) and then through the park, but in 1796 this last part was stopped up and the road was diverted to follow the north wall of the park, joining the Hockliffe-Newport Pagnell road at the north end of Woburn.

In 1839 it was proposed to turnpike the road from Woburn to Leighton Buzzard (passing the Fox and Hounds and through Heath and Reach) but this came to nothing.

Many stage coaches passed through Woburn carrying both mail and passengers. In 1818 Stephen Dodd, then the postmaster, wrote:

'On this Office much duty devolves, and that at very unseasonable hours; the Bedford cross post arrives at half-past nine with letters from the counties of Huntingdon, Hertford, Cambridge, Norfolk, Rutland etc. which are transposed into bags for Scotland, Ireland and all parts of the north; the London letters are forwarded by the Chester mail about eleven, and those for Dunstable, St. Albans, and Barnet, by the Manchester mail, which brings letters from the north about half-past eleven. The Chester mail arrives from London at two in the morning, with the London bags for this town and Ampthill, the latter of which is forwarded at five, with those to and beyond Bedford, by the man-mail, which brings letters from the north about half-past eleven.

The box closes at nine. Letters after that time, till half-past nine pay one penny; from half-past nine to ten, two-pence; and after ten sixpence.

Hours of delivery — from the 5th of April to the 5th of October, at seven o'clock, and during the winter quarter at eight.

There is no attendance at the office during divine service on Sundays, viz. from half-past ten to one in the forenoon, and from two to five in the evening.'

Most coaches called at the Goat Inn and each had its own name. By 1839 *The Unicorn* between Leicester and London called every day at 2.00 to London and 12.30 to Leicester; *The Express* and *The Courier* both went between Leeds and London, the *Express* at 9pm to Leeds and 1pm to London and the *Courier* at 10.30pm to Leeds and 10.30am to London; *The Victoria* went from Leighton Buzzard to Bedford via Ampthill passing through Woburn at 8.30pm every night to Bedford and 6am every morning to Leighton Buzzard. Other passenger services went to Oxford (coming from Cambridge) every Tuesday, Thursday and Saturday at 2pm; to Cambridge (coming from Oxford) every Monday, Wednesday and Friday at 2pm and to Wellingborough every afternoon at 2pm. A coach to Northampton also called at the Magpie every afternoon at 5pm. Several carriers are also listed going variously to London, Bedford, Olney, Newport Pagnell, Leeds and Nottingham from the Black Horse, White Hart, Goat Inn and in one instance from the carrier's house in the Market Place.

The *Royal Mail* from Derby and Halifax to London called at the Post Office every morning at 2.30 am and returned from London every night at 12.30am. Letters from Bedford also arrived by mail cart at 11.15pm and were despatched at 4am (the Chester Mail was listed in 1824 but not in 1839).

However, a note below these times says that by the time of publication some of the coaches would have ceased to run — a sign of the times, for below this note are details of the London, Birmingham, Manchester Railway which passed through Leighton Buzzard. By 1850 all had in fact changed, for no coaches were listed, but the Bedford to Bletchley branch of the London and North Western Railway had opened, and an 'Omnibus' from the Bedford Arms took passengers to the station at Woburn Sands to meet every train. Carriers continued to be listed until 1914 when there was only one left — Arthur Whiteman — who went locally to Bedford, Leighton Buzzard, Dunstable and Luton.

Until a few years ago a modern coach service between Nottingham/Northampton and London run by the United Counties Bus Co used to pick up passengers in Woburn several times a day on what must have been a similar route to that of the horse-drawn coaches. But, like the stage coaches of yesteryear, these too have passed away and the nearest stopping place is at Hockliffe on the Milton Keynes/London route. The local 'bus service No 141 Aylesbury-Bedford-St Ives has also diminished and now runs only every other hour instead of every hour.

ABOVE: The Duke of Bedford's coach and horses, 1800, (MTTBE) and BELOW: the Duke's coach c1830. (MTTBE)

ABOVE: The Duke of Bedford's coach and horses in Belgrave Square, towards the end of the 19th century. Alfred Lane's father is the coachman. (AL) BELOW: Park Street facing west in 1832. On the right is a waggon outside the Rose and Crown. A pencil drawing of 1832. (BM)

A great bonfire to celebrate the coronation of George V and Queen Mary in 1911. Over the years a number of these fires were built to celebrate Royal and other important events. (NH/RH)

The Social Scene

In 1612 there was reference to bear-baiting at Woburn church and there was probably bull-baiting too. A short distance from the west door of the Town Hall is an ancient iron ring set in stone; this is known as the Bull Ring. Tradition says that it was used for pulling down oxen for shoeing before they continued on the long march to London, but it may also have been used for bull-ring baiting.

Woburn at one time had a group of Morris dancers for, on Whit Tuesday in 1767, Parson Cole of Bletchley noted in his diary that 'Morrice Dancers from Woburne' visited Bletchley.

Another tradition, Maypole dancing, is referred to by the Churchwardens in their accounts for 1618: 'Paid for our dinners at Todington when we went about the poores' accompt and the Ryott about the May pole'. In 1672 a blacksmith's apprentice was charged with theft and incidental evidence in the court case revealed that on May day morning he had stuck May bushes at the doors of several people in the town; in his defence the minister and others of Woburn sent a certificate of good character to the Assizes, saying that at the supposed time of the theft the apprentice had been 'drinkinge and makinge merry at those houses where the May bushes were formerly stuck as aforesaid'. May customs lasted longer in Woburn than in many other places in the county, and maypole dancing was reintroduced in the late 1960s at the request of the then Vicar, Rev Terence Wenham. The author designed and made the maypole and his wife the ribbons: sixteen, each two inches wide for practice, and sixteen, each six inches wide for public performances. The author also made a portable maypole for the school, whose pupils are still carrying on the tradition.

Over the years a number of bonfires were built to celebrate Royal and other events. One such was made in 1911 for the coronation of George V and Queen Mary.

The materials used at the fire in 1911 were fifty-one cart loads of wood, and twenty gallons of paraffin. A watchman took charge for two days and nights. The Duke of Bedford provided the wood and local farmers transported it to the site with their horses and carts free of charge. Two barrels of beer were consumed. The Duke subscribed £20 towards the celebration funds.

The Institution played an important part in the social life of the town in mid-19th and early 20th century. So also did the Cottage Garden Society which held a giant annual show and was something of a successor to the old Woburn Holiday. Fruit, vegetables, flowers, lace, honey etc were exhibited in three marquees. However support declined and by 1912 the committee felt that they could no longer accept responsibility for the event without promises of more financial support. The Society struggled on for a few more years but eventually ceased, probably hastened by the First World War. A Garden Produce Association was formed later in this century and in conjunction with the British Legion held a show/fête for some years from 1947, but this too has ceased.

Woburn seems to have had an abundance of clubs and societies, particularly in the 19th and early 20th century. These included Woburn Dramatic Society; Woburn String Band; Coal Club; Sick Man's Friend; British and Foreign Bible Society; Glee Singers and Harmonic Society; Rifle Club; Temperance Society and Band of Hope; Freemason's Lodge; RAOB Lodge; Woburn Birthday Club, all of which are now extinct. Football, darts, bowls, tennis and of course cricket were all played with some success in local leagues.

Cricket has been played in Woburn since at least the 18th century, for the 4th Duke (1710-1771) hosted All England Cricket matches in Woburn Park and, on at least one occasion, served venison roasted on a spit for lunch. Lord Charles Fox Russell, who was a keen cricketer and in 1835 became president of the MCC, said that the Woburn Cricket Club first played in Woburn Park on 1 August 1777. Certainly successive Dukes of Bedford supported the club with donations and provision of kit at various times, and the cricket pitch in the park was improved in 1867. When funds fell really low in 1906 a deficit was made up by the Duke to keep the club in existence. During the 1936 season 'bats of suitable size' were provided for children under the age of 18, because the keen youngsters found the full-size cricket bats difficult to handle. A fund was set up and closed when enough money had been raised to buy four bats and three balls (about £6). The war years called a halt, when the ground was requisitioned by the RAF. However, it was started again some years after the war and a team still plays today.

Inns and taverns have always been meeting places for the people, some used commercially as coaching and posting inns as well as places for public meetings and court sessions. For a small market town Woburn has had an incredible number of inns. More than 30 names can be found in various registers and records of the past 300 years or so, but today only six remain. Quite a number were probably destroyed in fires while others were demolished and a few have been converted into private houses.

The White Hart is the earliest recorded, in one of the Russell documents dated 1635; the Woolsack occurs in 1650; the Horseshoe in Moore's survey of 1661; the Crosskeys in 1679; the Saracens Head in Assize Records of 1681; the Wrestlers in 1691; the Falcon in 1698; the Three Pots in

1711; the Wheatsheaf mentioned in Russell records of 1724 stood at the south end of Buck or Back Lane near the Town Hall. Buck Lane was once a thoroughfare running from the Town Hall, behind the shops and out into Bedford Street where the 'bus stop is now. A number of businesses and shops were in the lane, all of which were demolished at the end of last century. The Plough occurs in 1733 and the Blackbirds in 1741. A *Commercial Directory* of 1785 lists only five inns (which do not include the Wheatsheaf) — The Cock, the White Bear, the Black Horse, the George, which was the posting inn and the Goat, which was also the excise office. However, by 1823/24 the number had increased considerably and a directory of that year lists four inns (Cock, George, Goat and Magpie) and 12 taverns, which include the Wheatsheaf once more. Of these sixteen, only six now remain to serve the 800 or so inhabitants of Woburn and visitors. Population was at its greatest in the middle of the 19th century at about 2,000. Since then there has been a gradual fall until the beginning of the 20th century, since when it has been fairly stable. With the decline in population went the decline of the inns and taverns, especially after the loss of coaching trade, when the railway came to Woburn Sands.

Sixteen public houses were named in 1823/24. They included the Windmill, which has been found mentioned in 1806 but not in any directory after 1824; the White Lion which is now a private house, No 4 Bedford Street; the White Horse, now No 31 Leighton Street (maypole dancing used to take place in the field at the rear of the White Horse and circuses also performed there); the Shoulder of Mutton, now No 6 Leighton Street. The Bear is mentioned in the survey of 1661. It was in the High Street, but by 1785 there was the White Bear in the High Street — presumably the same place — which does not appear in any directories after 1823/24. The Cock appears in records as early as 1692, standing in what was then called Cock End. It was demolished in 1832 and houses of Georgian architecture were built on the site at Nos 18 and 20 George Street. Rev R.H. Moss, MA lived there as a curate until he himself became Vicar. The Goat dates back to at least 1650. In 1661 it was described as a 'Tenement or Inne beinge good howse of fower bayes, a brewhowse a stable and barne, cont six bayes with a garden orchard'. It was rebuilt in 1724 and was one of the principal inns of the town, being a coaching inn and an excise office. It is now a butcher's shop, in Bedford Street. The Rose and Crown used to be in Park Street at the rear of the present Sandon Saddlery. The Rising Sun stood in George Street at the junction with Duck Lane. Its deeds date back to 1733 and it was described as a hostelry, providing stabling for the horses of travellers. Pew No 12 in the old church went with the leasehold. Mr Higgins was the last proprietor and it was demolished in the 1930s. The site is now the garden of a house in George Street and apparently pieces of coloured glass are still frequently dug up. The Greyhound stood at the west side of what is No 1 Leighton Street and belonged to a brewery at the back of the house. For much of the 19th century it belonged to the Fowler family who were brewers in Woburn for many years and who also owned a malthouse and the Birchmoor Arms as well as many other public houses in the area. The brewery was known as Woburn Brewery and the house as Brewery House. However, Henry Fowler was certified as insane on 10 April 1880 and the property was sold on 26 February 1881. The brewery and the Greyhound were demolished in 1898 when Mary, Duchess of Bedford, converted the house into a cottage hospital, which it remained until 1903 when the Duchess built the Woburn Clinic (now Maryland). No 1 Leighton Street is now a private house. The Birchmoor Arms first occurs in a directory of 1864 but little of its history has yet been found. It was sold at the same time as the Greyhound in 1881, together with the malthouse that stood in the field next to the two cottages to the north of the Birchmoor Arms, and 26 other public and beer houses. The Birchmoor Arms was described at the time as containing a taproom and bar, parlor with cellar under the kitchen, four bedrooms, yard opening to the road, wash house, stabling for four horses, also a brick and slated skittle shed used as stabling and a good walled garden in the rear. It stands today to the north of the town on the Woburn Sands road. Other inns listed in 1824 which still stand today are the Bell, the Magpie, the Blackhorse, the Bedford Arms (formerly the George) and the Royal Oak (formerly the Red Cow).

The Bell is mentioned in documents dated 1685 when the rent was 5s 10d. It is on the left in Bedford Street, entering Woburn from the north and is noticeable by its square bay window. It was formed from two cottages, another was added to it in recent years and there was once a brewhouse at the rear.

The Magpie is a little further up Bedford Street on the left. It has been much altered structurally inside to meet modern requirements, but on a bill of sale in 1825 it was described as 'All that well known old established Commercial Inn now in full trade known by the sign of the Magpie, situate in the High Street Woburn . . . The house comprises a large Dining Room, two Parlours, Kitchen, Bar and exceeding good ale and wine cellars, with twelve comfortable sleeping rooms, compact yard, with stabling for twenty horses, Chairse House with excellent Granary over same, Brewhouse with a pump of exceeding good water, Wood and Coal Barn, and small cottage with a garden well planted with Fruit trees. The land tax is redeemed. The respectability and situation of these premises require no further remark, they are well adapted for Posting House or wine and Spirit Merchant'. It was sold for £1,650 on 31 August 1825.

The Blackhorse is mentioned in the Churchwardens' accounts of 1802. Pew No 8 in the old church went with the copyhold and there was a stable and a slaughterhouse at the back. Today it is a public house and a restaurant well situated in the centre of the town's High Street and is the only free house in Woburn.

The George is mentioned as far back as 1692. It was renamed the Bedford Arms in the middle of the 19th century and has always been an important inn. It used to be the focal point of social life, assemblies, balls, race meetings, quarter sessions, and petty sessions were held there. Three assemblies were held there each year and an annual statute session was held for the hiring of servants. At one time there was accommodation for fifty horses and twenty two coaches and it is said that teams of reserve horses were always harnessed up ready for when the coaches arrived, to avoid delay. The old stabling was rebuilt in 1836 and blacksmiths, farriers and wheelwrights were kept on the premises. The inn was once said to have been haunted by an old man and his dog, supposed to have been the hog keeper, who was burnt to death in his room in the fire of 1724. When the hotel was involved in structural changes in 1971 some skeletons were dug up. The Red Lion was probably attached to or very near the old George Inn because it is recorded that 'at Mich. 1775, Robert Martin entered upon the Red Lion Inn in Woburn at £20 per annum of the Revd. Mr. Williams, part of the house was pulled down and the remains laid to the George Inn'. Rumour has it that Guy Fawkes often stopped here to replenish himself and his horse on his frequent journeys between London and Gayhurst.

The Royal Oak was apparently called the Red Cow until 1774. It stands in George Street to the south of the town and was probably well away from the various fires. It is a picturesque old building still with a thatched roof. At one time it had its own brewhouse at the rear and its copyhold included seating in the old church — 'pew twentynine Woburn church south Aisle, pew number ten under South Gallery in the same church in which his servants sit.'

Order of Proceedings.

- **11.0** Service appointed for Coronation Day in the Parish Church.
- **1.30** The Band to play on Market Hill.
- **2.0** The Inhabitants meet on Market Hill, sing "God save the King," and go in procession to Woburn Park, headed by the Band and the Committee.
- **3.0** Athletic Sports, &c., in Woburn Park.
- **4.0** Free Tea for Children under 14.
- **5.0** Free Meat Tea for all the other Inhabitants.
- **8.45** Buns for Children.
- **9.0** "God save the King."
- **9.30** Fireworks in Wayn Close, followed by Bonfire.

God Save the King!

CORONATION

Of Their Most Gracious Majesties

KING GEORGE V.

AND

QUEEN MARY.

WOBURN.

Thursday, June 22nd, 1911.

Programme of events to celebrate the coronation of King George V and Queen Mary in 1911. (CJR/SR)

LEFT: The ancient ring among the cobble stones at the west end of the Town Hall. It may have been used for bull baiting and for tethering oxen while they were being shod. (A) RIGHT: No 4 Bedford Street, once the White Lion and later the home of Mr Maydwell. (A) BELOW: Playing bowls c1930, left to right — W. Deacon, H.D. Harris, ?, W. Maydwell, B. McKay, Mort Mattthews, Philip Hall. Douglas Harris alternated between bowls and tennis, which is why he is dressed in white. (GIH)

ABOVE: Houses built on the site of The Cock, George Street. (A) LEFT: This was once the Goat Inn, Bedford Street, now a butcher's shop. (A) RIGHT: No 1 Leighton Street, built in 1724, stood next to the Greyhound and its brewery and was known as Brewery House until the late 19th century, when the brewery was pulled down. Duchess Mary then converted it into a cottage hospital, which it remained until she built the Woburn Clinic (now Maryland) in 1903. It is now a private house. (A)

Name	Earliest reference found in other sources	1785	1824	1839	1850	1854	1864	1877	1894	1914	1920	1940
White Hart	1635											
Woolsack	1650											
Horseshoe	1661											
Cross Keys	1679											
Saracens Head	1681											
Wrestlers	1691											
Falcon	1698											
Three Pots	1711											
Plough	1733											
Blackbirds	1741											
Cock	1692	demolished in 1832										
White Bear	1661											
Windmill	1806											
Goat	1650											
White Lion												
Wheatsheaf	1724											
White Horse												
Rose and Crown												
Shoulder of Mutton							demolished in 1898					
Greyhound								demolished in 1930s				
Rising Sun	1733											
Blackhorse					Bedford Arms							
George	1692											
Magpie												
Bell	1685											
Royal Oak (Red Cow)	1774											
Birchmoor Arms												

Date of Directory

The rise and fall of inns and taverns in Woburn, based on a selection of commercial directories. (A)

A VALUABLE FREEHOLD PROPERTY,

COMPRISING

THE SUBSTANTIALLY BRICK-BUILT AND SLATED

MALT HOUSE, AT WOBURN, BEDS.

Consisting of 35-Quarter Steep, with ample stowage for barley; two Cemented Working Floors; double Kiln, with Wire Plates, Stokeholes, and capacious Malt Lofts beyond, with MALTSTER'S COTTAGE and piece of Ground at side.

YARD, and detached MALT CHAMBER of two floors

ALSO

A COTTAGE, occupied by a Servant of the Brewery.

AND

The "BIRCHMOOR ARMS," Public House,

fronting the Newport Road, containing Tap Room and Bar, Parlor, with Cellar under, Kitchen, and four Bed Rooms; Yard opening to road; Wash House, and Stabling for four horses; also a brick and slated Skittle Shed used as Stabling, and

GOOD WALLED-IN GARDEN IN THE REAR.

☞ *The Malt House and Premises connected therewith, as also the two Cottages, are* IN HAND. *The Public House is let to* Mrs. STONHILL, *at the low rent of* £13 *per Annum.*

THE WHOLE FORMS A COMPACT AND DESIRABLE ESTATE.

ABOVE: The Rising Sun, demolished in the early 1930s, with Mr Higgins in the doorway. It stood at the junction of George Street and Duck Lane and its site is now a garden. (PC) BELOW: The sale of the Birchmoor Arms and Malthouse in 1881.

ABOVE: The Birchmoor Arms today. Note the bricked-in windows on the side of the building. (A) BELOW: The Bell in Bedford Street almost opposite the almshouses. (A)

ABOVE: A group outside the Magpie, celebrating the relief of Ladysmith, Mafeking and Kimberley. Alfred Dawborn, the Woburn birdcatcher, is on the left. (L-L) BELOW: The Blackhorse in Bedford Street, the only free house in Woburn. (A)

ABOVE: Proprietor Puddephatt in 1876, outside the main entrance in George Street of the Bedford Arms, (L-L) and BELOW: unemployed men rolling the courtyard of the Bedford Arms early this century. (L-L)

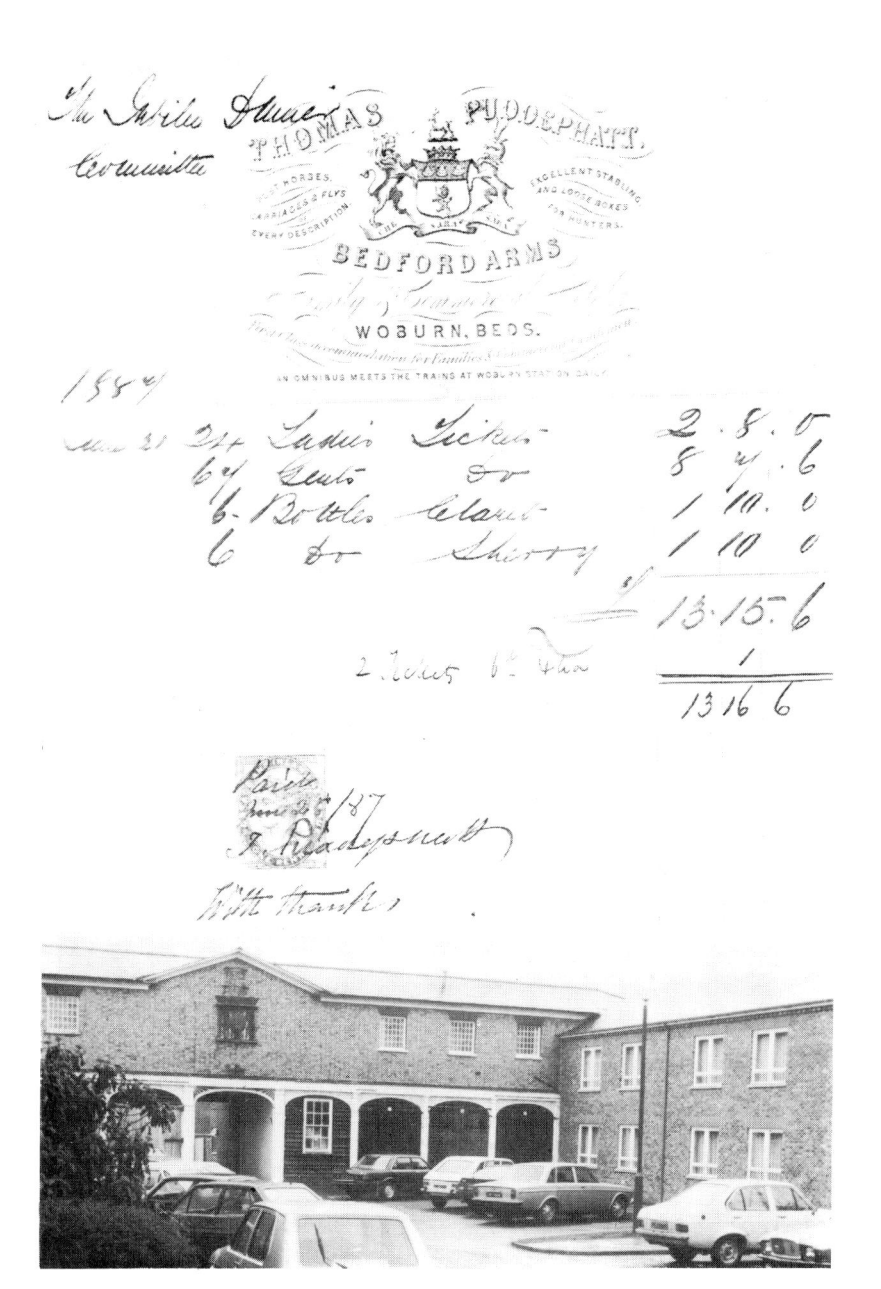

ABOVE: A bill for a Jubilee dinner in 1887, signed by T. Puddephatt. (L-L)
BELOW: The courtyard of the Bedford Arms today. (A)

ABOVE: Outside the Royal Oak c1900; the Rising Sun can be seen in the background. (L-L)BELOW: Cecil (Curly) Purser thatching the Royal Oak in the mid-1950s. (P)

Yesterday and Today

Woburn is surrounded by countryside and parkland. The Parish lies in the Manshead Hundred of Bedfordshire in the shape of a flattened pentangle with its western side on the county boundary. A belt of Lower Greensand stretches from Leighton Buzzard to Sandy and takes in the north western part of the parish with boulder clay in the south eastern section which contains two patches of Lower Greensand in the north east. There is a sub-soil of gravel. The parish lies between the 300' contour line in the north and the 500' line in the south with the village itself just below the 400' contour line and the Abbey with some of its ground just above it. Many parts of the parish are thickly wooded.

The Dukes of Bedford have had a considerable interest in forestry, agriculture and estate management, since the mid-18th century. The 4th Earl began the draining of the Fens in the 17th century but it was John, 4th Duke (1710-1771) who bought land to extend the estate and whose farmlands were among the most productive in England. He also started experiments which became the basis of 20th century forestry. Francis, 5th Duke, was called the 'Farmer Duke' and he was a leader in agriculture of the late 18th century. All kinds of experiments were conducted at Park Farm including the effects of different diets on sheep in 1794 and on cattle in 1797. In 1801 the Bedfordshire Agricultural Society was formed with the Duke as its first president. It was during his time that Park Farm was built in about 1780 to the design of Robert Salmon and Henry Holland. By the end of the 18th century the model farm was well established; Woburn Agricultural Society was founded (a forerunner of the Royal Agricultural Society) and Woburn Sheepshearing in June was an international event.

John, 6th Duke (1766-1839) was an influential landowner and as keen an agriculturalist as his older brother. In 1807, there was a Northumberland seed-drill at Woburn Park Farm which could drill seven rows at a time, a Mr Runciman of Woburn had a horse-hoe (at a time when most was still done by hand) and the Duke had a cast-iron drill-roller. The 6th Duke became Governor of the English Agricultural Society in 1838. Francis, 7th Duke (1788-1861) was a pioneer of land drainage and during his time the Woburn estate increased in size. The Ampthill estate was purchased in 1842. The 8th Duke did not spend much time at Woburn but Hastings, 9th Duke (1819-1891) was an ardent agriculturalist, succeeding Albert, the Prince of Wales, as President of the Royal Agricultural Society in 1879. In 1873, a government survey showed that the 9th Duke was the largest landowner in Bedfordshire with 33,589 acres, and the Beds-Bucks estate reached its peak in 1877 with 37,186 acres. As far back as the Hearth Tax of 1671, the largest nobleman's house in Bedfordshire was Woburn Abbey, rebuilt by the 4th Earl, with 82 hearths. In the 1850s experiments on feeding cattle were carried out at Woburn Park Farm for the agricultural research establishment at Rothamsted and in 1876 the Duke founded a permanent experimental farm at Woburn. Its director was Augustus Voelcker, under the Royal Agricultural Society. It is still doing valuable research work today and since 1926 has been run by Rothamsted. The Bedfordshire Agricultural Society still continued, and in October 1856 held its annual show and dinner at Woburn. The Bedforshire Architectural and Archaeological Society was formed in 1847 with the Duke of Bedford and Earl de Grey as joint presidents. It lasted until 1886. The process of buying land and property begun by the 4th Duke continued until the 20th century but the depression, and taxation during this century led to the break-up of many old estates, earlier in Bedfordshire than in many other counties. Property has also had to be sold from the Woburn estate, but in 1968 it was still the largest in the county at 12,620 acres.

The park consists of some 3,000 acres, enclosed by 11 miles of brick wall and is a sanctuary for many species of animals and birds. These include nine species of deer with the largest breeding herd of Père David deer in the world. It was Herbrand, 11th Duke, (1858-1940) who introduced the herd into the park from the imperial herd of China in 1894, saving them from extinction. He and his wife Mary built up a diverse collection of birds and animals, considered by some to be the finest collection of wild life in Britain outside Regent's Park Zoo. The Duchess was keen on game-shooting and fishing and had a particular interest in birds. She used to encourage the young boys of Woburn to study birds and trees by paying all expenses for groups of them to spend several days bird-watching in Scotland, and she sometimes accompanied them.

On the left just after entering the Park via Lion lodge are the Evergreens, over 100 acres of shrubs and rhododendrons which were planted in 1743 by John, 4th Duke of Bedford, to commemorate the birth of his daughter Caroline (later Duchess of Marlborough). In a book of 1839 entitled *Pinetum Woburnense* the then Duke of Bedford wrote that after a few years the 4th Duke thought that the shrubs needed thinning. He told his gardener how and where to thin them but the gardener did not wish to do so in case it spoilt the young plantation and also spoilt his reputation as a planter. However, the Duke insisted and put up a board facing the road which was inscribed 'This plantation has been thinned by John, Duke of Bedford, contrary to the advice and opinion of his gardener'. The subsequent growth of the plantation proved he was right.

To the north in the Park, concealed among the rhododendrons and shrubs is a delightful little thatched building known as the Thornery.

It was designed by Humphrey Repton and built in 1808. The roof is capped by a lantern light, the walls are of Tottenhoe stone and around the sides of the building are vertical tree trunks, which in part support the structure and in part are for decoration. It became delapidated but has now been completely restored. It was used by the Flying Duchess as a retreat and has been used by the family for picnics.

Also hidden among the shrubs is a picturesque 'hut' of logs built in the 'backwood style' and known as the Log Cabin. It was built about 1838 for John, 6th Duke, and the walls are made of logs with the windows and upper part of the door diamond leaded. This too has been completely restored. Neither of these buildings is open to the public.

Another building of interest in the Park is Paris House. This was built in prefabricated sections for the Paris Exhibition in 1878. It is in Tudor style and the Duke of Bedford brought it back to Woburn. At one time it was used by Duchess Mary as a hospital, affectionately known locally as the 'Tonsil Hospital'. Then a pilot, who rescued her from the desert when her 'plane came down, lived there until she died. At the beginning of the Second World War the Queen Mother's brother lived there and George VI and Queen Elizabeth (as she was then) often spent the weekend there during the war. General de Gaulle stayed there for a time too. Later it was lived in by senior estate staff and is now a restaurant.

The Abbey itself has been visited by private appointment for the past 200 years but it was opened to the general public in 1954. It is perhaps the most popular stately home in the country, visited by many thousands of people from all over the world. It houses a magnificent collection of works of art — furniture, silver, porcelain and paintings — and has been described as the 'most sumptuous jewel in the Bedford crown'.

The wild life of the Park was further augmented when part of it was made into a Wild Animal Kingdom or Safari, adding to the attractions for visitors and the preservation of this heritage, which has for so long been part of the Russell family.

The height of Woburn's prosperity as a market town was in the mid-19th century with a population of 2,049 (census of 1851). Trades offered in a directory of 1850 included four bakers, three butchers, three blacksmiths, four booksellers/stationers, four boot and shoe makers, one brewer, three cabinet makers and upholsterers, two carpenters and joiners, four chemists and druggists, two china and earthenware dealers, one coal merchant, two corn dealers, six grocers/tea dealers, three linen and woollen drapers with two Berlin wool repositories, two maltsters, three milliners and dressmakers, three painters and plumbers, two saddlers and harnessmakers, three straw bonnet makers, four tailors, a wheelwright, clockmaker, gunsmith, stonemason, brazier and tinman, animal and bird preserver, hairdresser, toy dealer, fishmonger, cooper, timber merchant, several insurance agents, two auctioneers, a coroner, a solicitor and ironmonger. Where Marquess Court now stands there was an engineering works and iron foundry owned by William Hensman & Son, who made agricultural implements. When they moved to Ampthill the buildings were used by Gibson Andrews to store builders' supplies. There were still 11 taverns and Baptist, Methodist and Congregational Chapels were much in evidence as well as the Parish Church. Petty sessions were held every fortnight, there was still a weekly market on Fridays and four fairs were held in January, March, July and September — altogether a busy, thriving town.

However, within 50 years the population had fallen by half to 1,129 at the turn of the century in 1901. This was partly due to the railway coming to Woburn Sands and taking away much of Woburn's commercial trade and through traffic. During the 20th century there has been a continuing, but slower, fall in population with 800 inhabitants recorded in 1981.

Alfred Dawborn was known as the Woburn Birdcatcher, and lived in the thatched cottage next to Maryland, which became known as Birdcatcher's Cottage. His job was cutting and tying hay, ditching, hedgecutting and gardening, but he spent a good deal of time catching wild birds to sell. Caged birds were always to be seen hanging outside his house and he was a familiar sight standing by them in his smock and billycock hat. He was born in 1820 and died in 1919 just before his 100th birthday. He had thirteen children: six daughters and seven sons. Most of his daughters went into private service when they became of age, one of his sons, William, worked for Lord Charles Fox Russell and two sons joined the army and died of fever in India. Some years after his death the cottage was used as a home for nurses who worked at the hospital nearby. Today it is a private house.

The present Reject China Shop used to be an ironmonger's run by Gibson Andrew. An old range supplied by the firm used to be in the old almshouses.

There has not been a baker's shop in Woburn for many years now but the Lilley family had one in Bedford Street; Robert James Lilley is listed in a directory of 1850, and Edward in 1920.

William John Maydwell came to Woburn when he was about 12 years old. He was one of a family of five sons and one daughter. His father was a master tailor who had the reputation of being the 'finest cutter of his day' and worked for John Mckay Brothers at their drapery business on the Market Square. William followed his father's trade, working for Mr W.G. Hulatt as a tailor in premises that once stood on the green opposite the Town Hall. He later worked for himself at his home in Bedford Street until he was over 80 years old, sitting cross-legged on the table. In 1957 he received the Maundy Money from Queen Elizabeth II at St Albans Abbey, the first time the ceremony was held outside London. William sang in the church choir for about 80 years. He died at the age of 92.

The Ames family used to run a garage at the rear of the Bedford Arms. Alfred Ames was once employed by Herbrand, 11th Duke, as head mechanic. He was in charge of the Duke's motor-car drivers, who had to be mechanics as well as drivers in case of breakdown. The Duke had a fleet of cars and Alfred estimated that while he served the Duke the fleet included 10 Daimlers, 10 Napiers, one Rolls Royce, one Argile and a steam car.

The estate's interest in forestry meant that a timber yard was a useful commodity and it still exists in Gas Lane. Many years ago the woodland around Woburn was an attraction to botanists and lily-of-the-valley bloomed in profusion. It is still one of only two main areas in the county where the flower may be found growing wild. Apparently in the 18th century lily-of-the-valley from Bedfordshire used to supply the London markets, and Parson Cole of Bletchley wrote on 3 June 1766, 'Tansley went to Aspley Wood for some Lillies of the Valley' and on 7 June 1767, 'Tansley went, as usual, to get me some Lillies of the Valley'. The soil in parts of Aspley and Woburn was attributed with petrifying qualities in early printed accounts, supposedly due to the extreme coldness caused by a petrifying spring. It was said that a wooden ladder which had been converted to stone was kept in the monastery of Woburn and posts had been dug up whose lower parts were completely petrified.

No official Parliamentary enclosure took place in Woburn but by the time of Moore's map in 1661, piecemeal and private enclosure by the Duke had taken place — most of those field boundaries still exist.

The town today has the overall appearance of an extremely attractive Georgian village. In an appraisal by the County Planning and Conservation Department, Woburn is considered to be exceptional, even by national standards and the Council for British Archaeology has included it in its list of the most important historic towns in Britain. It is the quality and variety of buildings which give Woburn its character — the architectural styles range from the 17th century through Georgian and Victorian Gothic to the present — and many buildings are listed as of special architectural and historic interest. However, mid-19th century estate cottages and the Georgian style are dominant. The estate has been criticised by inhabitants over the years for an apparent policy of buying properties and then demolishing them. However, the standard of housing for labourers and tenant farmers was always ahead of its time and the estate considered that it was uneconomical to keep in repair old, defective housing. Instead, old houses were demolished and new, sound houses were built. Herbrand, 11th Duke, in particular was criticised in this way, but during his time new houses were built in Leighton Street, Speedwell, Crawley/Bedford Road, and on the site of the old Union Workhouse (London End/White City). Houses built by the Duke have a cipher on them of a 'B', a coronet and the date of building — there is even one on the corrugated wall of the swimming pool changing rooms in Crawley Road. Recently more new houses have been built in Duck Lane, Park Street, London End and Marquess Court off Bedford Street, most of them in a Georgian idiom so that the unity, and character of the village is preserved, with most dwellings clustered along the High Street, George Street, and Leighton Street and three small groups of houses at Birchmore, Speedwell and Pinfold.

The street scene and pattern have remained basically unchanged since before the 19th century, the crossroads having the Town Hall as a focal point and each street having its own character. Indeed, it might be surmised that it is these crossroads which this century have caused Woburn to become and remain a small village. When the Abbey was established the hamlet grew in importance and size until the mid-19th century. But when the coaching era gave way to the railway and omnibus, things began to change, for the railway went to Woburn Sands, Bletchley and Leighton Buzzard and with it went the traffic, jobs and facilities needed to support the coaches. The coming of the motorway M1 took many heavy lorries away from the village's traffic, leaving Woburn as a place to pass through *en route* rather than stop at unless for a specific purpose.

The street pattern may not have changed but the variety of trades offered by the shops has done so dramatically. Only a butcher, a grocer and the post office provide the everyday needs of the village people and the nearest bank is at Woburn Sands. There is a boutique, ladies' dress shop, bookshop, china shop, hairdresser, restaurant, tea shop and wine bar, otherwise the shops sell gifts and antiques mainly for people from the surrounding area, or for the visitors who come in large numbers from all over the world to visit the Abbey, and its parkland.

And so Woburn survives to please its citizens and visitors, retaining a serenity and dignity that are not often found in this modern age. The wheel has turned full circle. First springing up at the gates of the monastery, the village and then town prospered through the centuries. Now it has returned to the size of the quiet country community it was in the 17th century, with the Abbey still influencing its affairs.

Lion Lodge at the entrance to the park, near the parish church in Park Street. (A)

ABOVE: Woburn Sheepshearing. An engraving dated 31 May 1811 by George Garrard. (BCRO/MTTBE) BELOW: London Gate or Entrance, designed by Henry Holland and built in 1790. It is between Woburn and Hockliffe on the road to London taken by the coaches. (MTTBE)

IMPORTANT TO AGRICULTURISTS

WHEAT SOWING.

DOWN'S FARMERS' FRIEND.

UNDER THE DISTINGUISHED PATRONAGE OF

His Royal Highness the Prince Albert,

AND IS

USED ON THE ROYAL FARMS,

And those of their Graces the Dukes of Norfolk, Bedford, Devonshire, Manchester, Portland, and Sutherland; Marquises of Camden and Exeter; Earls Fitzwilliam, Talbot, Powlett, Spencer, Sandwich, Somers, Essex, Cowper, Clarendon, Gainsborough, Chesterfield, Lisburn, Brownlow, and Beauchamp: Viscount Campden; Lords Sondes, Alvanley, Braybrooke, Elphinstone, and Henniker; Baronets Sir J. Tyrrell, Sir W. Geary, Sir H. Hunloke, Sir G. Robinson, Sir W. Welley, Sir J. Nelthorpe, Sir E Lacon, Sir J. Palmer, Sir T. F. F. Boughey, Sir W. Kemp, Sir E. Bacon, Sir T. D. Legard, Sir W. Halford, Sir E. Vavasour, Sir C. Morgan, Sir W. D. Broughton, Sir E. Kerrison, H. N. Burroughes, Esq., M.P., Colonel Westenra, M.P., Major-General Wemyss, Colonel Bisse Challoner, Charles Barnett, Esq., Francis Pym, Esq., the Honorable George Ongley, and other eminent Members of the

ROYAL AGRICULTURAL SOCIETY OF ENGLAND!!

DOWN'S FARMERS' FRIEND is a sure and certain remedy for the SMUT IN WHEAT, and the ravages of the Slug, Grub, and Wireworm. It will promote the germination and growth of the Seed Wheat, and increase the produce of the crop quite equal to a change of seed.

From the Bailiff of His Grace the Duke of Bedford.
Park Farm, Woburn, Beds, September 15th, 1852.

Sir,—I have much pleasure in informing you the result of the Farmers' Friend I used last year on His Grace the Duke of Bedford's farm has been very satisfactory; I have seen no smut where it was applied.
Yours truly, G. W. BAKER.

PREPARED AT THE MANUFACTORY, WOBURN, BEDS,

IN PACKETS AT TENPENCE EACH,

ESTABLISHED 1864.

RETAIL CATALOGUE
OF NEW AND GENUINE

Agricultural, Garden, and Flower Seeds,
SOLD BY

THOMAS TOMPKINS,
WHOLESALE AND RETAIL

Seed Merchant & Grower, Colliery Agent & Coal Merchant,
BEDFORD STREET, WOBURN, BEDS.

Dealer in Corn, Hops, Cakes, Barley and other Meals, Soot, Artificial Manures, Hay, Straw, Potatoes, Roots, &c.

AGRICULTURAL SEEDS.

MANGOLD WURTZEL.

Carter's Champion, Yellow Globe, with a very small top and tap root, excellent cropper, per lb.	1/
Yellow Globe, ordinary heavy cropper ,,	9d.
Carter's Warden Mangold, very hardy ,,	9d.
Long Yellow do. ,,	9d.
Giant Mammoth, Long Red, as exhibited at Agricultural Show, 1874 ...per lb.	1/
Red Globe	9d.
Sutton's New Golden Tankard, Yellow Fleshed Mangold, a valuable novelty, partaking of the sacharine qualities of Swedes, or Yellow Turnips ...per lb.	1/6

SWEDE TURNIPS.

Essex Improved, Purple top, a splendid shape, and heavy cropper ,,	1/
Skirvin's Liverpool Swede, very hardy ,,	10d.
Skirvin's King of Swedes ,,	10d.
Hall Westbury's Purple top ,,	10d.
Carter's Champion Purple top ,,	1/
Sutton's do. ,,	1/
Minier's Improved—this stock has taken several prizes this last season ,,	1/
Bangholm Swede ,,	10d.
Provident Swede, the largest in cultivation ,,	10d.
Hartley's Bronze top ,,	10d.
Shepherd's Golden Globe ,,	1/
White Flesh Swede do. ,,	10d.

WHITE TURNIPS.

Stratton's Green Round, very hardy ,,	9d.
Pomeranian, White Globe, very fine stock ,,	9d.
Paragon, Red Globe, very fast growing, and early to eat off ...per lb.	10d.
Stone or Stubble ,,	10d.
Green Globe ,,	9d.
White Tankard ,,	9d.
Green Tankard ,,	9d.
Orange Jelly ,,	10d.

HYBRID.

Waite's Eclipse, a capital substitute for a Swede, with Purple top, very hardy, fast growing, and a heavy cropper ...per lb.	1/
Dayl's Hybrid ,,	1/
Yellow Scotch, or Bullock's Heart ,,	1/
Early Devon, or Grey Top Stone do. ,,	1/

KOHL RABI, or Turnip Round Cabbage.

A splendid stock of Improved Green, grown from large bulbs, and taken several prizes this season ...per lb.	1/6
Purple do. ,,	2/6

CARROT.

James' Intermediate, a very heavy cropper, a Red, Short, and Stubby Carrot ...per lb.	1/6
Altringham, red, heavy cropper, green top ,,	1/6
New large White Jersey Carrot, extraordinary heavy cropper ...per lb.	1/
White Belgian, Green top ,,	1/
Yellow Belgian ,,	1/
Marriott's Improved, Scarlet top ,,	1/6

PARSNIP.

Large White Guernsey ,,	1/6
Hollow Crown do. ,,	1/6
Student Parsnip, a very heavy cropper ,,	1/6

GRASS SEEDS.

Mixed, for Lawns, per lb.	6d.
Cocksfoot, per qr.	54/
Festuca, Meadow per cwt.	75/ to 100/
Red Festuca Rubra ,,	34/ to 48/
Foxtail ,,	80/ to 90/
Tall Oat ,,	45/ to 60/
Italian Rye Grass ,,	20/ to 40/
Timothy Grass ,,	45/ to 60/
Pacey Bents per qr.	28/, 34/, 48/

OPPOSITE: An advertisement of 1853, for an agricultural preparation made in Woburn used by members of the Royal Agricultural Society of England.
ABOVE: Thomas Tompkins' 19th century agricultural catalogue.

ABOVE: The Thornery, designed by Humphrey Repton and built in 1808; water colour of 1842 by J.C. Bourne, (MTTBE) and BELOW: the Log Cabin, built for John, 6th Duke, about 1838. (By J.C. Bourne/MTTBE)

ABOVE: Paris House, a prefabricated building made for the Paris Exhibition, afterwards erected in the Park; later a private residence, it is now a restaurant. (AB) BELOW: A pen and ink drawing by C. Rowland from a print of Woburn dated 1851. On the left is the building that is now the Boutique, and in the centre is the lane that used to pass behind the shops into Leighton Street (Buck Lane). The buildings on the right have been demolished and the 'bus shelter is there now. (CR)

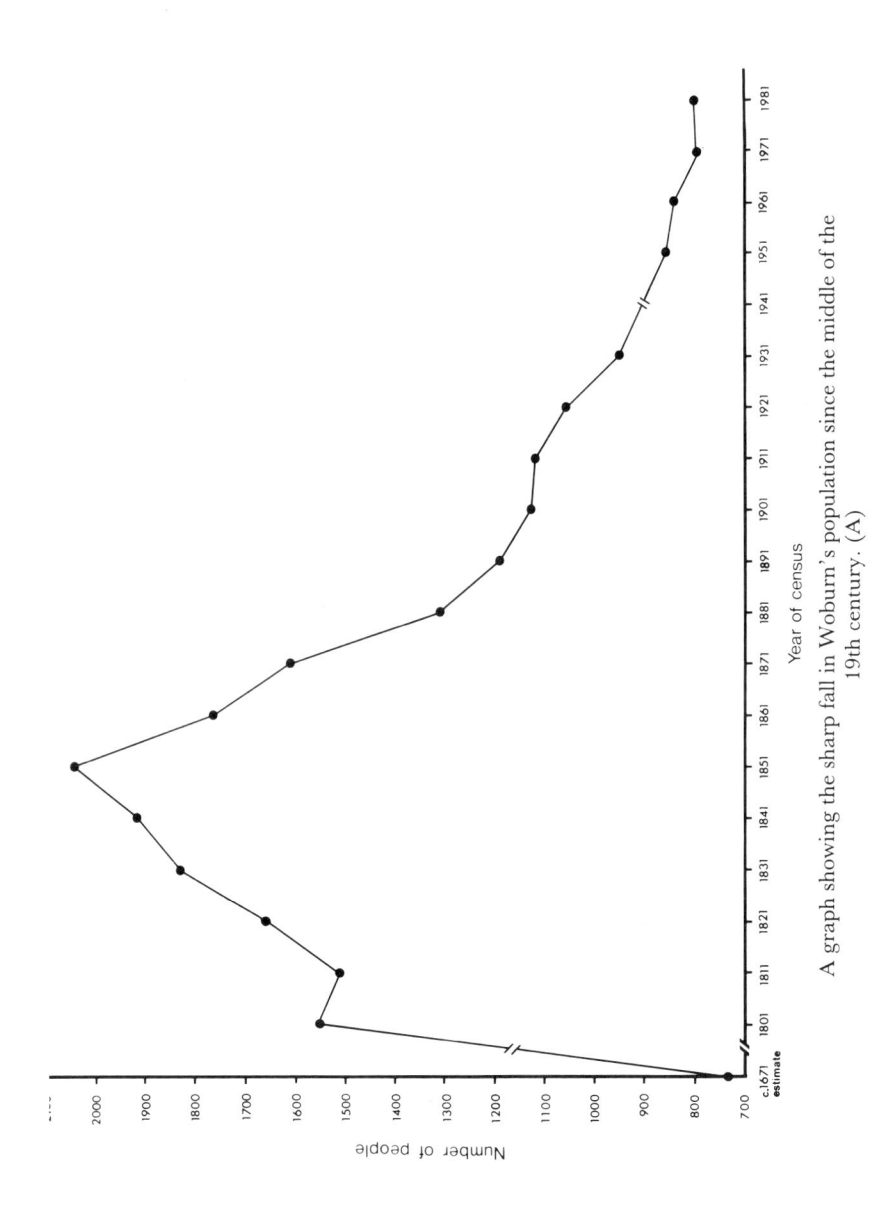

A graph showing the sharp fall in Woburn's population since the middle of the 19th century. (A)

Woburn Abbey, the west front, as viewed in the 1830s, (JDP) and today. (JW)

ABOVE: Turney's grocery shop with Mr Turney second from the left in the doorway. Today's art gallery retains the facade; (CS) LEFT: G.P. Turney's signature on an 1897 bill. (L-L) RIGHT: The shop that was once Boughton's Saddlery. The back of the Town Hall can just be seen on the right and the old church tower is in the distance. Buck or Back Lane used to pass from the centre of the picture, behind the main street shops and into Bedford Street. The Baptist chapel was in this lane. Today there is no through road. (A)

Boughton's Saddlery shop in Leighton Street behind the Town Hall; George Boughton, who served his apprenticeship in Luton, centre. Started before 1864, it closed in 1946. (BC)

ABOVE: A 1911 bill to the Woburn Coronation Committee, signed by G.R. Boughton. (L-L) BELOW: A once familiar sight, outside Sycamore Cottage, Bedford Street, 1970. (AB)

ABOVE: Alfred Dawborn, the Woburn birdcatcher, standing with his housekeeper outside his cottage. On the wall hang several caged birds; (AD) BELOW: Birdcatcher's Cottage until recently, when an extension was added to the left. (A)

ABOVE: The staff of Lord Charles James Fox Russell; William Dawborn, son of the Woburn birdcatcher, second from right. (AD) BELOW: Gibson Andrews, ironmonger's, in the Market Square 1930, the War Memorial took over its former crossroads site in 1920. Robert Hile, standing in the doorway, worked there for well over 40 years. (NH/RH)

ABOVE: The Reject China Shop was once Gibson Andrews; left is the gallery, once Turney's grocery shop. (A) BELOW: Gibson Andrew's bill to the Woburn Bonfire Committee in 1902 for coronation expenses. (L-L)

Order of Proceedings.

- 11.0 Service ordered for Coronation Day in the Parish Church.
- 1.30 The Band to play on Market Hill.
- 2.0 The Inhabitants meet on Market Hill, sing "God save the King," and go in procession to Woburn Park, headed by the Committee, the Band, and Decorated Cycles.
- 3.0 Athletic Sports, &c.
- 4.0 Free Tea for Children under 14.
- 5.0 Free Meat Tea for all other Inhabitants.
- 8.0
- 9.0 "God save the King."
- 9.30 Fireworks in Wayn Close, followed by Bonfire.
- 11.0 Torchlight Procession starting from the Ivy Lodge.

FISHER & SON, PRINTERS, WOBURN, BEDS.

God Save the King!

CORONATION
Of Their Most Gracious Majesties

King Edward VII
AND
Queen Alexandra.

WOBURN.

Thursday, June 26th, 1902.
Saturday, August 9th, 1902.

Dr. to E. LILLEY,
High Class Confectioner, Bread & Biscuit Baker.

Bride and Birthday Cakes to order.

ABOVE: The amended Woburn programme to celebrate the coronation of Edward VII and Queen Alexandra. (CJR/SR) BELOW: E. Lilley's bill to the Coronation Committee, 1911.

Miss Lilley outside her baker's shop, now a restaurant. (CR)

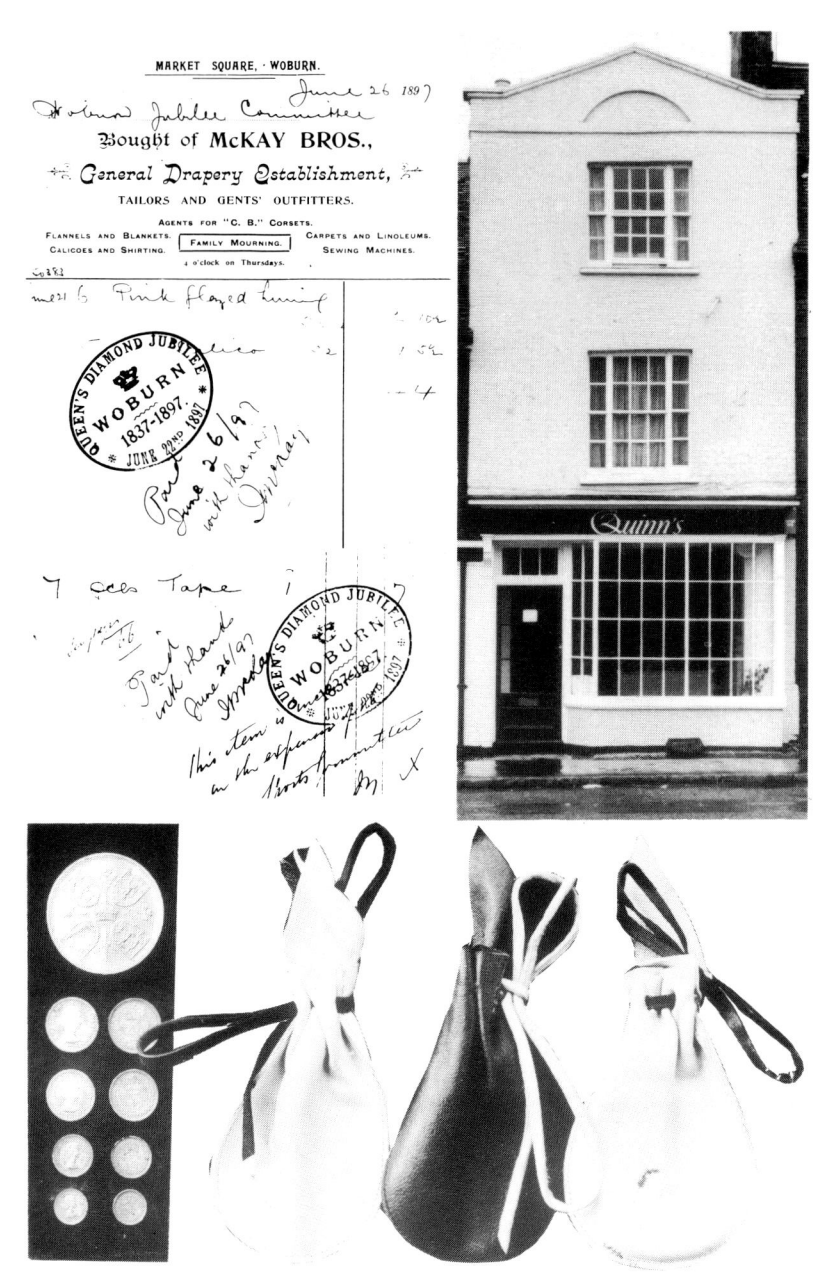

LEFT: R.J. Lilley's bill to the Queen's Diamond Jubilee Committee in 1897, (L-L) and RIGHT: Miss Lilley's shop, now a restaurant. (A) BELOW: Maundy Money presented to William Maydwell in 1597 at St Albans Abbey — the first time the ceremony was held outside London. He left it to Woburn church. (JW)

LEFT: William John Maydwell, tailor, holding the Maundy Money. (BT) RIGHT: A bill from McKay Brothers, employers of Mr Maydwell's father, to the Jubilee committee of 1897. (L-L) BELOW: John Gilby, Draper's 1897 billhead. (L-L)

No. 1

Motor Car Act, 1903.

COUNTY [~~or COUNTY BOROUGH~~] OF _Bedford_

Licence to Drive a Motor Car (or Motor Cycle).

Albert James Ames

of _Woburn Abbey_

Beds

Is hereby Licensed to Drive a Motor[a] _Car_ for the period of TWELVE MONTHS from the _1st_ day of _January_ 1904, until the _31st_ day of _December_ 1904, INCLUSIVE.

W.W. Marks

Clerk to the County Council ~~or Town Clerk, or duly Authorised Officer~~.

N.B.—Particulars of any endorsement of any licence previously held by the person licensed must be entered on the back of this licence.

ABOVE: The first driving licence issued in Bedfordshire, 1 January 1904 — to Albert James Ames, head mechanic to Herbrand, 11th Duke of Bedford. (JA)
BELOW: William Douglas and Jack Ames (left) with Jim Ames (right), outside the garage the Ames' brothers took over in 1919, in the courtyard of the Bedford Arms. (JA)

ABOVE: Jim Ames in his model T Ford outside his garage, 1920s; (JA) CENTRE: the Duke's Napier shooting brake 1920, (JA) and BELOW: Bill Timms and Jack Collins in one of the Duke's Napiers, c1920. (JA)

ABOVE: Unloading in Woburn timber yard; Ernest Peacock is behind the rear horse. (P) BELOW: Park Street from the crossroads, c1860. The sign of the Rose and Crown is on the left and Lion Lodge in the distance, at the entrance to the Park. Clarke's chemist shop is on the right, next to premises once behind Wiffen's (later Andrews') ironmonger's shop. (L-L)

IMPORTANT TO FARMERS!
THE BEST AND CHEAPEST DRESSING FOR SEED WHEAT
IS
D. CLARKE'S WHEAT PROTECTOR,

Which has stood the test of **SEVEN** years, and proved to be a **CERTAIN PREVENTIVE OF SMUT IN WHEAT,** and an effectual safeguard against the destructive attacks of the **SLUG, GRUB,** and **WIREWORM.** Prepared by

D. CLARKE, CHEMIST, WOBURN, BEDS,

In packets, 9d. each, sufficient for SEVEN bushels of seed. May be had of Chemists in every town in the kingdom.

The patronage and recommendation of the Royal Agricultural Society of Great Britain, the rapidly increasing sale of this article, and the hundreds of testimonials in its favor (similar to the following) received by the proprietor, are the best proofs of its efficacy.

TESTIMONIAL *from W. Anderson, Esq., late Bailiff to His Grace the Duke of Bedford.*

SIR, *Oakley, September 10th,* 1850.

I beg to inform you I have now had an opportunity of examining both the winter and spring wheats dressed with your preparation, and, in both instances, I am happy to say, *not one single ear of smut is to be found.* I can, therefore, with satisfaction recommend it to my brother agriculturists.

I am, Sir, yours &c.

☞ *AGENTS appointed on application to the Proprietor.* WALTER ANDERSON.

G. B. CLARKE,
OPERATIVE AND MECHANICAL DENTIST,

(Late Pupil of Mr. C. H. Smartt, Surgeon Dentist to the London Dispensary, &c., &c.,)

PARK STREET, WOBURN, BEDS,

Respectfully announces to the gentry and public of the county of Bedford, that he may be consulted on all matters connected with Dental Surgery and Mechanism.

TERMS STRICTLY MODERATE.—*Patients attended at their own residences if required, without extra charge*

☞ Mechanical Work executed for the Profession equal to any London House.

ABOVE: 1853 advertisement for D. Clarke, chemist and G.B. Clarke, dentist.
BELOW: No 11 Bedford Street, believed to be the oldest house in Woburn. (A)

ABOVE: The old thatched cottages at the end of Duck Lane gutted by fire in 1979, (AB) and LEFT; since rebuilt with tiled roof. (A) RIGHT: No 7 Bedford Street. (A)

ABOVE LEFT: No 12 Bedford Street; (A) RIGHT: Crowholt, once the home of Lord Charles James Fox Russell, son of the 6th Duke, and of Hastings, 12th Duke; (A) CENTRE: modern architecture at the junction of Duck Lane/Leighton Street. (A) BELOW LEFT: The Bedford Cipher, in Leighton Street, (A) and RIGHT: Marquess Court, off Bedford Street. (A)

Bedford Street facing south, c1850. Dodd and Peeling's office is now Woburn Post Office. On the right, the shop (now the Boutique) beside Buck Lane; (L-L) OPPOSITE: an advertisement by Dodd and Peeling in 1853, and BELOW: Woburn Post Office today. (A)

WOBURN BRANCH

Depository for the Society for Promoting Christian Knowledge.

DODD AND PEELING,

BOOKSELLERS,

Printers, Bookbinders, Stationers,

ETC., ETC.,

POST OFFICE, WOBURN,

Beg to call particular attention to the BOOKBINDING Branch of their business, and solicit the favor of a trial from those who have not yet patronized them, assuring them that they cannot be surpassed by any house in London or Country. The various styles of their

BOOKBINDING

Comprise Russia, Morocco, Vellum, Velvet, Silk, Calf, Roan, and Half-bindings, and ornamented in the most modern and fashionable style.

MUSIC AND MANUSCRIPTS CAREFULLY BOUND.

PATTERNS IMITATED;

Old Books neatly repaired, relettered, and polished, which, at a trifling expense, will preserve them for a considerable length of time.

Every description of PLAIN and ORNAMENTAL

Stationery at the Lowest London Prices;

5 quires of Full size Cream Laid or Blue Wove Note Paper for 1s.; good serviceable ditto, 5 quires for 1s. 6d.; superfine Thick Satin, 4s. 6d. per 10 quires; the old-fashioned Hand-made Paper, 4s. 6d. per 10 quires.

ENVELOPES OF EVERY DESCRIPTION.

CRESTS, DIES, INITIALS, AND DEVICES Engraved and Stamped upon Note Paper and Envelopes at a trifling extra cost.

Engraving and Letter-press Printing

IN THE FIRST STYLE OF THE ART.

Address Copper-Plates Engraved and 100 Superfine Cards Printed for 4s. 6d.

THE CHEAPEST PAPER-HANGINGS

IN THE COUNTY are to be had at DODD AND PEELING'S. A piece of 12 yards for 4½d. Sitting Room Papers 6d., 8d., 9d., and 1s. per piece. Bed Room, Marble, Granite, Ceiling, Oak, and every other description of Paper-Hangings equally low.

GUTTA PERCHA PAPER FOR DAMP WALLS.

D. and P. can strongly recommend this Paper, as they have tested it for three years with success where every other preventive materials have failed.

ABOVE: The Market Square facing south, c1880, with the present Town Hall (right), Andrews' ironmonger's shop (left) next to the Bedford Arms, (CJR/SR) and CENTRE: c1930, the war memorial is on the site of buildings in the previous picture, but those on what is now the green are still standing; BELOW: today, the Town Hall (centre right) and the Blackhorse on the extreme left. (JW)

ABOVE: Bedford Street facing north c1900, with the old Parsonage (left) and Blackhorse (right); (CJR/SR) BELOW: Bedford Street today, by Brian Cairns. (MC)

ABOVE: Bedford Street facing south c1900, with the railings of the old churchyard (right); (CJR/SR) CENTRE: the Market Square facing east to Park Street from Leighton Street c1880, with Andrews' (right); Fisher printers, (left); (EH) BELOW: facing north c1900 — the spire has been removed from the parish church. (CJR/SR)

ABOVE: The Market Square facing east, (CJR/SR) and CENTRE: facing north, (both) with the same policemen and gentleman in a hat; (CJR/SR) BELOW: Market Square today, drawn by Brian Cairns. (MC)

LEFT: The mortuary chapel and the old church tower are now Woburn Heritage Centre which is cared for by a Board of Trustees. The building houses a museum of local history. RIGHT: Inside looking towards the entrance. Christine Pohl is on duty. BELOW: The Village Hall, opened in 1987, the Committee in 1999.

Into the Millennium

My father, Kenneth G. Spavins, began writing *The Book of Woburn* and it was my pleasure to complete it following his sudden death in 1982. Published in 1983 on subscription, demand was such that non-subscription copies soon sold out. Ever since there have been regular enquiries but no new books available. Seventeen years later I am delighted that the book is reprinted with new material to the millennium and I hope you enjoy reading the continuing story of Woburn's history and traditions. I should like to thank the trustees of Woburn Heritage Centre and, in particular, the Trust's chairman, Gill Green, whose encouragement and support have made the reprint possible.

There have, of course, been changes since the book first appeared, and later research has identified one or two errors of fact. Since it would be impractical to amend the text, this second edition concludes with a look back from a millennial vantage point, embracing many of the changes since 1983. At the same time, illustrations charting change and recalling aspects of Woburn not originally covered follow the text. Page and paragraph follow each addendum, arranged chapter by chapter.

Many Mansions:
After the mortuary chapel had been declared a redundant building in 1981, the Marquess of Tavistock approached the village with a proposal that the chapel be de-consecrated and that he should then give the building to the village as long as the village was responsible for its repair. The alternative was demolition.

A committee was formed in the village and money raised through grants, public subscription and fund-raising events. The chapel and tower were put in good order and are now Grade 2* listed. In 1984 the building was named as Woburn Heritage Centre and The Woburn Heritage Centre Trust was formed with ten trustees, whose aim was to care for the building and to offer it for public use. The late Arthur Bayntun, the Centre's first curator, gathered objects and photographs of local interest and created a museum of local history in the main part of the old chapel. Colonel Tony Fowle, the first chairman, raised funds through local grants and, by registering the Centre with the Thames and Chiltern Tourist

Board, was able to make the transept into a Tourist Information Point. The Heritage Centre is manned entirely by volunteers and opens every day during the summer months. Entry is free and the Centre relies on donations and sales of maps, walk leaflets, books and other items for income. Around 7,000 visitors, some local and some from all over the world, visit the Centre each year and in 2000 the Trust received £30,000 from the Heritage Lottery Fund to improve the building, by glazing the open sides of the tower base and converting the old bell-ringers' chamber in the tower into a resource room. *(page 37/para 5)*

In 1994 the Heritage Centre organised the first Woburn Village Open Gardens Day with around 15 gardens in the village open to the public. With refreshments served at the church and a plant stall at the Heritage Centre, this has become a popular annual event. Other fund-raising events include an Easter Art Exhibition, participation in the Oyster Festival and, at Christmas, 'Madrigals, Mulled Wine and Mince Pies' with songs provided by the Heritage Madrigal Singers.

In 1994, the Trustees of the Woburn Heritage Centre decided to fund the complete overhaul of the Vulliamy clock by Smith of Derby. At the same time, an automatic winder was fitted, much to the delight of Bill Bayntun, who previously had wound the clock manually twice a week! The only public clock in the village, it strikes the hour and keeps excellent time. *(page 41/below)*

The mortuary chapel is now the museum of the Woburn Heritage Centre. *(page 44/below)*

Private Means and Public Works:
In September 1994 Eddie Cheeseman, the then landlord of the Black Horse, persuaded the landlords and owners of the other pubs and restaurants in the village to get together for one Sunday in the year to celebrate an oyster day. The shops and villagers became involved and the Woburn Oyster Festival was born, with a seaside theme, a mermaid and sand on the Pitchings. The Oyster Festival is now held every September and has grown to include a Friday night Concert on the Pitchings, a Saturday Antique Flea Market and fun and music on Sunday, with thousands of oysters (plus other food and wine) consumed. As Woburn is just about as far from the sea as is possible in England, the Festival's eccentricity and growing reputation are a cause of much surprise and amusement. Any profit from the Festival goes into a fund for the youth of the village. A hard-surface multi-play area has just been built beside the village hall and in 2000 the money will help refurbish the open-air swimming pool in Crawley Road.

(page 47/para 3)

The old pound was removed when the houses were built in Timber Lane in 1992. *(page 47/para 2 et seq.; page 58/below)*

1990 was the 700th anniversary of Queen Eleanor's cortège from Grantham, where she died, to Westminster, where she was buried. Tony Fowle, the then chairman of the Woburn Heritage Centre Trust, researched the history of the time, hoping to discover just where the Woburn Eleanor Cross stood, but with no success. We should like to think it stood on the corner of Park Street on the site of the War Memorial. In 1990 Arthur Bayntun made a replica of the cross, similar to the one that stands in Waltham Cross today. The model and an exhibit about the crosses can be seen in the Heritage Centre. *(page 48/para 2)*

The Town Hall is no longer used for recreation. The ground floor at the front of the building is an Antiques Centre and the upper floor and rear offices are auction rooms. The Village Hall, completed and opened in 1987 in Crawley Road by public subscription, fund-raising events and much free labour from the community, is now the recreation hall and meeting place for the village. *(page 48/para 3)*

In 2000 there are 47 pupils at the school. In recent years, it has at times been at the full capacity of 52. *(page 52/para 1)*

A new Fire Station in George Street was opened by the Marquess of Tavistock in 1998. The old Fire Station in Leighton Street now houses classic cars for wedding hire. In 1999 the concrete hose-drying tower in London End, behind the old station, was proposed as a mobile-phone tower. The proposal was defeated and the tower has now been demolished. *(page 53/para 4)*

Gas Lane is now called Timber Lane because the timber yard was there until recently. In 1992 forty-six houses were built on the site for private sale. The Marchioness of Tavistock took an active interest in the design to ensure that, although inside the houses were modern, their exterior blended with the Victorian brick cottages in that area of Leighton Street. The occupants of the houses, plus other new building, have increased the village population from around 750 in 1983 to over 1,000 today, bringing additions to the school register and new life to the community. *(page 56/para 1)*

When 45 Bedford Street, next door to the school, was refurbished in 1990, an old Woburn Gibson-Andrew range was removed from the house and is now in the Heritage Centre museum.

(page 63/below)

The Dissenters:
The Congregational chapel was demolished in 1986 and the two houses known as Amhurst Court, off Duck Lane, were built on the site. Thirteen houses were built in Howland Close and Bloomsbury Close, off London End, in 1979–80. *(page 98/above left)*

In 1993 the Methodist chapel was converted into a private house.
(page 98/above right)

Woburn's Wheels:
Over recent years the 'bus service through Woburn has diminished. In 2000 there are just seven buses each way between Leighton Buzzard and Milton Keynes each day, Monday to Saturday. There is no service on a Sunday. *(page 106)*

The Social Scene:
The maypole is still used today. *(page 109/para 3)*
    In the last few years a bonfire and fireworks display have been held to celebrate 5 November. The event is currently held on the old recreation ground in Timber Lane and in 1999 attracted between 600 and 800 people. *(page 109/para 4)*
    In 2000 several clubs and societies still meet in Woburn. The WI Woburn Branch has just celebrated its 75th anniversary, and has 28 members, who meet in the Village Hall; so do the Wednesday Social Club, a Mothers and Toddlers and Play Group, Weight Watchers, Aerobics and a thriving Brownies pack. Also in the village there is a Madrigal Group which meets once a week and gives occasional concerts, including one each Christmas at the Heritage Centre. *(page 110/para 2)*
    Sadly the cricket club folded in 1992. *(page 110/para 3)*
    The butcher's shop on the site of 'The Goat' closed in 1987. Since then the building has been an antiques shop, an oriental gift shop and is now a specialist motoring bookshop.
(page 111/para 2 & page 115/left)
    The Birchmoor Arms became an Indian restaurant in the early '90s but is now a pub once more, renamed 'The Birch'.
(page 112/para 1)
    In the late '80s two private houses opposite the Bell Inn were converted and extended to form the Bell Hotel with 23 rooms.
(page 112/para 2)

Yesterday and Today:
In 1984 the Greensand Ridge Walk (GWR) was opened. It is 40 miles long and stretches across Bedfordshire from Leighton Buzzard in the south west to Gamlingay in the north east. The waymark sign for the GWR is a muntjac, the small 'barking' deer from Asia that the 11th Duke introduced to Woburn Park in the late 19th century and which has now spread throughout the surrounding counties, causing problems to farmers and gardeners alike. *(page 123/para 1)*
    In the mid '80s the Reject China Shop was renamed the Woburn China Shop, no longer selling rejects but stocking all the leading

brands of china and glass. Their summer and winter sales are legendary and a queue is to be seen in Bedford Street every Boxing Day morning waiting for the winter sale to begin. *(page 126/para 4)*

Gas Lane is now called Timber Lane. *(page 127/para 2)*

Over the past 30 years traffic, especially heavy lorries, has increased dramatically, with currently some 700 to 800 trucks pounding through the village every weekday. The fabric of the old village was not intended to take this kind of hammering and, since January 1973, a Traffic Committee has been campaigning for a weight restriction on vehicles passing through Woburn. In 1990, the County Council deferred a decision until the A5 Little Brickhill by-pass had been built. When that was completed, the Council came in 1995 to the point of imposing a lorry weight limit, only to postpone the decision once more, at the eleventh hour, this time until the projected eastward extension of the Leighton–Linslade by-pass could be completed. At the time of writing, there is no funding provision for this work. The village therefore looks set to bear its disproportionate burden of heavy lorries, and the noise and damage they cause to old buildings by vibration, for the foreseeable future. *(page 128/para 2)*

In 2000 the butcher, dress shop, book shop and wine bar have gone but, in addition to the pubs and restaurants, antique and gift shops, there is now a flower shop, a kitchen shop, a specialist motoring book shop and 'The Country Cross-Stitcher', which draws enthusiastic cross stitchers from a wide area. *(page 128/para 3)*

London Gate is now the entrance to The Paris House restaurant. *(page 129/below)*

In 2000 the population of Woburn is just over 1,000. *(page 134)*

Turney's grocery shop is now The Flower Shop. *(page 136/above)*

Boughton's Saddlery is now a Kitchen Shop. *(page 137/below)*

The Reject China Shop with the gallery to the left are now Woburn China Shop and The Flower Shop respectively.

(page 141/above)

William Maydwell's Maundy Money is now on display in the Woburn Heritage Centre, on loan from the Parish Church. Mr Maydwell received the money in 1957, not 1597 as the caption suggests! *(page 144/below)*

List of Incumbents:
The Reverent Paul Miller retired in 1998 and was succeeded by the Reverend Alan Heslop in 1999. *(page 158)*

As the century turned, the Parochial Church Council discussed ideas for a project to mark the millennium and it was decided to restore the red altar frontal. It is Victorian, richly embroidered and bejewelled, but the brocade is badly worn and torn in places. Many fund-raising activities have been organised, co-ordinated by Frances Spavins (the author's widow and my Mother) who herself had previously remounted the jewelled embroidery of the white altar frontal in 1977. The Marchioness of Tavistock has taken a keen interest in the project and offered to buy the materials.

In the village the millennium will be marked by the planting of a tree, with a circular seat around it, on the Pitchings behind the Town Hall. The war memorial at the corner of Park Street is to be cleaned and the village sign, erected for the Festival of Britain in 1951, renovated. A plaque will also be added to the sign to mark Woburn's twinning with the town of Bedford, Virginia, USA, a settlement begun by the 4th Duke of Bedford in 1754.

Thus Woburn enters the millennium with a growing population. Some traffic and other environmental threats exist, but there is a thriving sense of community and strong retail presence, its appeal is undiminished and its heritage intact.

ABOVE: New housing development on the site of Timber Lane. INSET: The Bedford Cipher on the side of one of the houses built on the development site next to Timber Lane (compare with the Cipher shown on p 151). BELOW: Woburn Post Office on a warm sunny day in the summer of 2000.

ABOVE: The front of Woburn Lido — swimming for all hides behind its facade!
BELOW: People relaxing and bathing there.

ABOVE: Looking south towards the War Memorial and gable end of the Bedford Arms Hotel. The locally famous summer sale at Woburn China Shop is in full swing next to The Flower Shop. Road works are in progress. LEFT: Formerly the Goat Inn, the building is now a specialist motoring bookshop. The shop sign over the entrance in the photograph on p 115 now hangs in the Heritage Centre. RIGHT: Formerly the Woburn Country Shop (see p 136), the building now houses York House Interiors. The wooden posts in the 1983 photograph have been replaced with more robust metal ones in a slightly different alignment. Notice in the centre of the photograph that the old bull ring remains in place (see p 114).

ABOVE: The front of The Bell Inn has changed since 1983 (see p 118). BELOW: Formerly The Birchmoor Arms, then an Indian restaurant, today The Birch is a pub once more. Now boasting an extensive porch to the front, the lower side windows which are shown bricked up in the photograph from 1983 (see p 118) are opened up, letting in light to the ground floor.

APPENDIX 1
List of Incumbents

Designated in the registers as ministers, curate, pastor, clerk and since 1868 as vicar:

1558 Samuel Walpoole		
1564 John Barker		
1587 John Johnson		
1595 Oliver Pigge	Died	1594
1600 Caesar Walpoole		
1609 Harmand Sheppard		
1616 Zacheens Breedon		
1659 William Blagrave	Ejected	1662
1667 Robert Marshall		
1674 William Marshall	Died	1704
1715 Daniel Newcom		
1722 — Bristed		
1733 John Evans	Resigned	1761
1761 — Morris, B.D.	Died	1798
1800 John Parry, MA	Died	1823
1823 Thomas Roy, MA	Died	1834
1834 Henry Hutton, MA	Resigned	1848
1848 Hay MacDowell Erskine, MA	Resigned	1853
1853 Emilius Bayley, MA	Resigned	1856
(afterwards Sir Robert Laurie (Baronet))		
1856 Samuel Francis Cumberlege, MA	Resigned	1874
1874 Henry Willes Southey, MA	Resigned	1900
1900 Charles Russell Dickinson, MA	Resigned	1912
1913 Reginald Herbert Moss, MA	Resigned	1915
1916 A. Verner G. White, MA	Resigned	1929
1930 Brian C.C. Pratt, MA	Resigned	1932
1932 Frederick A. R. Harvey	Resigned	1937
1937 Henry Martindale, MA	Resigned	1941
1946 Thomas N. Gunner	Resigned	1961
1961 Robin O. Osborne, BA	Resigned	1965
1965 John T. Wenham, MA	Resigned	1971
1971 Andrew Bradley, OBE	Resigned	1975
1975 J. Ralph Deppen, NB, MDR, STD, DD, formerly Archdeacon of Chicago U.S.A.	Retired	1978
1979 Paul Richard Miller, BSc, AKC, Priest-in-charge, Vicar from 1st March 1980		

APPENDIX II

The Earls and Dukes of Bedford

			Relationship to previous Earl or Duke
John,	1st Earl	*d*1554/55	
Francis,	2nd Earl	1527-85	son
Edward,	3rd Earl	1572-1627	grandson
Francis,	4th Earl	1593-1641	cousin
William,	5th Earl & 1st Duke	1616-1700	son
Wriothesley,	2nd Duke	1680-1711	grandson
Wriothesley,	3rd Duke	1708-1732	son
John,	4th Duke	1710-1771	brother
Francis,	5th Duke	1765-1802	grandson
John,	6th Duke	1766-1839	brother
Francis,	7th Duke	1788-1861	son
William,	8th Duke	1809-1872	son
Hastings,	9th Duke	1819-1891	cousin
Sackville,	10th Duke	1852-1893	son
Herbrand,	11th Duke	1858-1940	brother
Hastings,	12th Duke	1888-1953	son
John,	13th Duke	1917	son

Bibliography and Other Sources

Bedford, John Duke of, *A Silver-Plated Spoon,* London (1959)
Blakiston, Georgina, *Woburn and the Russells,* Constable (1980)
Davis, F., *Luton Past and Present,* (1874)
Dodd, Stephen, *History of Woburn,* (1818)
Dony, John G., *Flora of Bedfordshire* Beds. County Council (1969)
Dony, John G., *Bedfordshire Plant Atlas* Luton Museum (1976)
Emmison, F.G., *Turnpike Roads and Toll Gates of Bedfordshire* Beds. Hist. Rec. Soc. Survey III (1936)
Godber, Joyce, *Friends in Bedfordshire and West Hertfordshire* Luton and Leighton Monthly Meeting (1975)
Parry, J.D., *History of Woburn* (1831)
Pevsner, Nikolaus, *The Buildings of England. Bedfordshire and the County of Huntingdon and Peterborough* Penguin (1968)
Scott-Thomson, Gladys, *Woburn Abbey and the Dissolution of the Monasteries* Transactions of the Royal Historical Society (1933)
Scott-Thomson, Gladys, *Life in a Noble Household 1641-1700* (1937)
Steele Elliott, J., *The Pounds of Bedfordshire* Beds. Hist. Rec. Soc. Survey III (1936)
Viatores, *Roman Roads in the S.E. Midlands* V. Golancz (1964)
Victoria History of the County of Bedford Ed. H. Arthur Doubleday & William Page, F.S.A. (1904- '12)
Wiffen, J.H. *Historical Memoirs of the House of Russell* London (1833)
Commercial Directories of 1785, 1823-24 (Pigot & Co.), 1839 (Pigot & Co.), 1850 (Slater), 1854 (Post Office), 1864 (Post Office), 1877 (Post Office), 1885 (Kelly), 1894 (Kelly), 1914 (Kelly), 1920 (Kelly), 1940 (Kelly).
Bedfordshire County Record Office
Bedfordshire County Council Planning Department
Bedfordshire Magazine
Bedford Office, London. Archivist Marie P.G. Draper.
Luton Museum. Archivist Marion Nichols.
Notes of the Rev T.N. Gunner, Douglas Harris, Jack Humberstone, P.G. Ruffhead, Victor Chubb, Arthur Bayntun, Peter Summers, Mr Cecil Rhodes.

Key to Caption Credits

A	Owned by the author/Anne Applin/David Applin
AB	Loaned by Arthur E. Bayntun
AD	By courtesy of A.J. Dawborn
AL	Loaned by Alfred Lane
BC	From the Bagshawe Collection by kind permission of R.W. and N.T. Bagshawe
BCRO	By courtesy of Bedford County Record Office
BM	By kind permission of the *Bedfordshire Magazine*
BT	By courtesy of the *Bedfordshire Times*
CJR/SR	With thanks to C.J. and S. Rawlings
CR	By kind permission of Colin Rowlands
CS	By courtesy of Christopher Sykes Antiques of Woburn
EA	Loaned by Mrs Ethel Armsden
EH	Loaned by Mrs Evelyn Hobourn and given to the author's family after his death
EPE	By kind permission of the *Evening Post-Echo*
GIH	Loaned by G.I. Howard
JA	Loaned by Jack Ames
JDP	Taken from J.D.Parry's *History of Woburn* 1831
JJ	Loaned by Mrs J.M. Jardine
JR	By courtesy of John Rowland, Chief Forester 1955-68
JRA	By courtesy of J.R. Ashby
JW	By kind permission of John Walker
JW/V	Photo John Walker, by kind permission of the Vicar
L-L	By courtesy of Mrs Leigh-Lancaster (née Morrison)
MB	By courtesy of Bedford Museum
MC	By courtesy of Maryland College Woburn
MTTBE	By kind permission of the Marquess of Tavistock and the Trustees of the Bedford Estates
NH/RH	By courtesy of Nora and Robert Hile
P	Loaned by Mrs Purser
PC	Loaned by P. Cowlishaw
SA	By courtesy of Mrs Serena Aldous
SD	Taken from Stephen Dodd's *History of Woburn* 1818
WS	By courtesy of Woburn Lower School

Index

Figures in Italics refer to illustrations

Abbey, abbot of........16,17,18,19
   cellarers of........................18
   dissolution of 18,21
   Fountains.....................16,17
   St Albans........................17
   seal of 22
   Warden.......................18,19
   Woburn, passim
Ackworth, Yorkshire 100,101
Act, Charities......................54
   Education 51
   Mending of Highways.......103
advowson...........................29
Agricultural Society,
   Bedfordshire..............123,124
   English 123
   Royal......................123,124
   Woburn 123
Albert, Prince of Wales.........123
Albrett family.....................54
Albright, William 100
Alric, thegn 15
almshouses 47,49,54,*63,64*
altar, of Lady Chapel.............73
   of new church 34,72,73,74,
                                     82,83
   of old church 34
   rails 72
Ames, Albert James.............146
   Alfred *121,127*
   James *146,147*
   family 126,*146*
Ampthill.........19,21,47,100,105
                                        123,126
Andrews, Gibson......*63*,126,*140,*
                                   141,154,156
annals, entries in..................17
Aragon, Catherine of.............19
Aspley Guise 55,100,101
Aspley, charter 15
   Lane 29
   Wood 127
Aumbury............................73
Avis, Mrs...........................74
   Sydney 77
Aylesbury 106

Back (Buck) Lane....111,*133,137*
Baker, Sarah 100
Balls, Joan 50

band, church 33,34
   ringing 76
Baptists.......................99,100
barrel organ........................33
Battlesden................55,74,104
Bear, The 111
bear baiting......................109
Bedford 105,106
   cipher *151*
Bedford Arms, The.105,112,*120,*
                   *121,*126,*146,154*
Bedford Street..31,53,54,111,112
      *114,119,*126,127,*138,149,*
          150,151,152,155,156
Bedfordshire....16,18,20,103,127
   Architectural & Archaeological
     Society........................124
   Association of Church Bell
     Ringers 77,78
   Association of Change
     Ringers.......................*94,*
                                95,96
   County Education
     Department..................51
belfry 76,77,*92,95,96*
Bell, The 112,*118*
Bell Man (Town Crier) 48
Bells, clock *44*
   sanctus 31
   of old church 76,77,90,*91*
   of new church ...71,76,77*91,92*
Benedictine, Abbey at York....16
bibles 73
Birchmore, church of....16,29,37
   parish of 29,30,*38,38,39,*47,
                           54,124
Birchmoor Arms, The..........112
                                 117,118
   House................ 53
Birdcatcher's Cottage.....126,*139*
Blackbirds, The 111
Blackhorse, The.....105,111,112,
                        119,154,155
Bletchley 109,127,128
Blore, Edward....34,48,*57,58,*79,
                                    97
Blunham, Dan Laurence 20
Bolebec, Hugh de 15,16,18
                                 29,*89*
bonfires................*108,*109,*141*
Boughtons's Saddlery shop ...*136,*
                                      137

Boughton, G.R. *136,138*
Bowden, Mrs..................54,*64*
bowl, silver..........................*14*
bowls................................*114*
brewery, Woburn 112,*115*
Brickhill, Bow....................100
   Little 100
British Legion....................110
Brown, Polly........................*60*
Bryan, Sir Francis............20,21
Buckingham Palace 48
Buckinghamshire 16,21,22,50
bull baiting..................109,*114*
Bull Ring 109,*114*
Burleigh, Miss J. *62*
bursar 18

Cage 49
Cambridge........................104
candlesticks 73,74,*83*
Carey, Robert, surgeon 79
Caroe, W.D. 72
cars *146,147*
Chambers, Sir William .32,34,78
chancel 31,71,72,73
chandelier 35
chapels, Baptist 99,100,126
   Congregational *98,*99,126
   Lady 72,73,74
   Methodist..............*98,*99,126
   Mortuary............31,37,*43,*54,
                      72,73,77,*97*
chapel-of-ease..........29,30,31,37
Charity Bread 78
Charles I............................52
   II 53
Chenies 21,22,71
Chernock, Sir John 100
Chester 103
Chichester, Ralph de........... 48
choir 72
   stalls 72
Christmas figures *14*
Church goods, list of..............32
   temporary wooden 37
   Woburn new 30,37,71
      et seq, *80,81*
   Woburn old........30,31,32,34,
      36,37,*40,43,*72,73,79,
               109,111,126
churchwardens 32,33,50,53

173

churchwardens' accounts 32, 34,48,53,109,112
churchyard *43,97,156*
Cistercian, abbot 16
  abbey..........................16
  foundation at Woburn 16
  Order..........................16
Citeaux..........................16
Civil War........................52
Clare, James................55,*64*
Clarke, D.................*148,149*
Clinic, Woburn 56,99,112,*115*
clock, church tower 32,35, *43*,77
clubs and societies ......109 et seq
Clutton, Henry 36,48,72
coach, Duke of Bedford's *106, 107*
  modern service 105
  stage 104,105,106
Cock, The..................111,*115*
Cole, Parson 127
Collins, Jack......................*147*
communion plate 34
Congregationalists................99
Cottage Garden Society 110
County Fire Service...............54
Crawley Road 127
cricket..........................110
Cromwell, Thomas 19
cross 48,72,74,*83*
Cross Keys, The 110
Crowh*o*lt *151*
crypt. 71,*81*
Cumberlege, Rev Samuel Francis......................*40*,78

Dawborn, Alfred.....*119*,126,*139*
  William.........................*140*
de Gaulle, General..............125
deer, Pere David 124
Derby 105
Dickinson, Rev Charles Russell 73,77
directories *116*,125
Dom Ralph Barnys 29
Dodd, Stephen 31,34,48, 53,104
  and Peeling *152,153*
Domesday Book 15,*24*
Douglas, William *146*
Duchess, Adeline 72,*81*
  Georgina 34
  Mary (the 'Flying Duchess') 56,*69*,73,112,*115*, 125
Duck Lane 111,127,*150,151*
Duke of Bedford, 1st.........32,53
  4th.............32,54,110,123,124
  5th.........................33,123
  6th 34,35,*42*,48,123,125
  7th..........................35,123
  8th................36,37,71,123
  9th 48,123,124

10th.............................72
11th 48,53,72,73,76,124, 126,127,*146*
13th............................22
'Duke's door' 72
Dunstable 105

Earl of Bedford, 1st 22,*27*
  2nd...........................49,50
  3rd 54
  4th 22,49,54,123,124
  5th 53
Eaton Socon 50
Edgar............................15
Edmonson, Mrs G.H.............73
Edward the Confessor 15
Edward I 17
  VI 22
  coronation of................*142*
Eleanor, Queen 48
Elizabeth, I 30,49,55
  II 126
enclosure 127
Epping, Essex..................100
Espec, Walter 16
Eversholt 37.50,55,74

Fair, September 47,52,126
  March.....................47,126
  January 47,126
  July (Cherry) 47,126
  October (Statty or hiring).........................47
Falcon, The 110
Fermband, Sir Thomas 47
Figgis, Rev Patrick...............99
fire, first........................52
  second......................52,53
  third 53
  engine 53
  engine house..........51,54,*62*
Fisher, Bishop 19
Flitwick 17
Flying Horse Farm 104
font, old church 34
  new church 34,72
Foots Cray, Kent 74
Fountains (Fontibus or Fontes),
  abbey of 16,17
  abbot of 16
Fowler, family 112
Fox and Hounds 104
frankpledge....................17,18
  view of 18

gallery 35
Garden Produce Association .110
Gas Lane 47,49,56,*58*,127
gas lights........................56
Gayhurst 113
Geoge, The.........*57*,111,112,113
George, V 109,*113*

VI 125
George Street..........48,111,113, 115,120,128,*151*
Giffard, Walter.................15,16
Gilby, John....................*83,145*
Goat, The 105,111,*115*
Goodwin, Thomas..............100
Grace, John......................21
Greathead, Rev Samuel.........99
Gresham, William 33
Greyhound, The.....111,112,*115*
Gunner, Rev T.N...........29,73, 77,79
Gurney, Thomas 51
Guy Fawkes 113

Hacket, Thomas 100
Halifax..........................105
handbell(s) 76,77,78,*93*
Handbell ringers..................76
Harding, Stephen 16
Harland, William 33
Harlington 55
Harris, Douglas 78,*96*,*114*
'Harry', poltergeist 113
hatchments (commemorative armorial plates)...........37,*89*
Hearth Tax......................124
Hedgecroft 29
Hendley, John 33,35
Henry, II 18
  III 17,30,47
  VIII 18,19,21,47
Hensman, William & Son 125
Herbert, Charles 76,77,78,*95*
  Cyril 78
  Ernest 77,78
Higgins, Mr....................111
High Street..................37,78
Hill, Humfrey...................50
Hitchin 100
Hobbs, Robert, Abbot 18,19, 20,21,*26*,30,31,*89*
Hobourn, family.................73
Hockliffe 55,99,103,104,106
Hogsty End....................100
Holland, Henry 30,123
horse-hoe......................123
Horse Shoe, The 110
hospital, cottage 56,*69*,*115*
  'Tonsil' 125
  Woburn Abbey War.........56
housing 127
Howland, Mrs Elizabeth 51
Hulatt, W.J. 77,126
Hulcote 55
Hundreds, map *25*
Husborne Crawley 15,49,55
hymn board......................74

Independent, Congregational 99
inns, taverns........110 et seq,*116*

174

Institute, Woburn Mechanics 49
Institution, Woburn Literary & Scientific 49,110

James I...............................30
Job's Farm 15
Keens, Francis 48
Kempe, J.E. 72,73
King's College, Cambridge 71

lace-making 50,*60*
Langston, Mr 'Steff'.............99
Leeds................................104
Leicester...........................105
Leighton Buzzard 15,17,47,48 49,52,56,99,105,123,128
  meeting house 99
  Street............15,49,51,53,56, *58,69,98,*99,100,111, 112,*115,*127,128,*133,156*
Liber Regis 30
library 49
Lidlington 54
lights, electric 56
  gas 56
lily-of-the-valley 127
Lilley, Edward 126,*142*
  Miss *143,144*
  Robert James............126,*144*
Lincoln registers 18
Lion Lodge 124,*148*
Log Cabin, the 125
London 19,22,34,103,104, 105,106,109,127
  End (White City).............53, 55,99,127
  Road 48
Lord's Mead, meadow..........30
Lowe, Thomas 21
Luton Mission Church 38

Magpie, The 105,111,112,*119*
mail coach...................104,105
Malthouse *117*
Manchester 105
manor, lord of.........15 et seq
map, 19th Century.............*46*
map 1901 ....*102*
market, Sunday 47
  weekday 47
  Woburn 47
Market House.............53,56,*57*
  place 105
  square 48,*57,58,*126, *140,154,156,157*
Markham, Gervase Prior........20
Martin, John 35
Marquess Court......125,127,*151*
Mary, Queen 109
Maryland, adult education college............49,56,69,*70,*99, 112,*115,*126

Maundy Money......126,*144,145*
May customs.....................109
Maydwell, William John.....126, *144,145*
Maypole dancing 109,111
McKay, John..............126,*145*
Mears and Stainbank............76
Memorial, War 56,*70,140,154*
Methodists 99
Miller, Rev Paul..................74
Milton Bryan 55,74,104
  Keynes 106
Missal stand 74
Moore, Sir Jonas 29,30
Moravians..........................99
More, Sir Thomas 19
Morris dancing 109
Morrison, H......................53
Morton, John 31
Moss, Rev R.H. MA......73,111

nave, old church 31
  new church 71,73
Newport Pagnell...53,99,104,105
Norman and Beard 73,74
Northampton 103,105
Northumberland seed-drill....123

oak tree 20,*26*
Old Warden 16
Olney 105
Omnibus 105
Organ, new church 35,72,73
  old church 37
organ loft 73,74,*82*
Overseers of the Poor........50,55

Paris House....................125
Parish Register 52
Park, the Abbey ......48,104,110, 123 et seq
Park Farm 48,56,123,124
  House, Old Warden..........36
  Street............71,79,*107,*111, 127,*148,156*
Parratt, Michael 54
Parry, J.D.........16,17,18,20,31, 35,51
parsonages........47,78,79,*97,155*
Paternoster Row 22
Peacock, Ernest................*148*
Petre, Dr 19
petrifying spring................127
pews 33,35,36,*43,*111,112,113
Pickering, Sir Edward...........30
  family 30
Pinfold.........................54,128
  Cottages *23*
  pond 17,*23,*49
  stream 15,*23*
plague 22,54
Plough, The 111
Pond, Drovers'...................49

Poor Law Union..................55
Pope, The 19.20.29
population......32,36,50,111,125, 126,*134*
post office...................105,*152*
Pottesgrove/Potsgrove 53,55,
Pound, the 47,49,*58*
Priory, Dunstable 17,18
Puddephatt, Mr *120,121*
pulpit, of new church........33,72
  of old church *33381*

Quaker schools *98,*99,100
Quakers (Scociety of Friends) 99,100

railways...........................126
Rectory 30
Red Cow, The 112,113
Red Lion, The..................113
Red Lodges.......................104
Reformation, The 32
Repton, Humphrey 125
reredos 72,73,*82,83*
Restoration, The 53,100
Reubens, copy of 74
Ridgemont 55,74,104
Rievaulx 16
Rising Sun, The 111,*117,122*
Robson, Thomas, organ...72,73, 74,*83*
Roman road 15
pottery 15
Rose and Crown, The ..*107,*111, *148*
Rothamsted, agricultural research establishment......124
Royal Oak, The......112,113,*122*
Runciman, Mr 123
Russell, Baron John 21,22,2⁷
  Lord Charles Fox 110,126, *140,151*
  Lord William...................53
Russell family 29,32,36,49, 54,71,125
Rye House plot 53

St Francis window............72,73
St Ives 106
St Mary the Virgin, Turnstall 73
Salford 55
Salford, Dan Robert........19,20
Salmon, Robert 33,34,123
sampler 51
sand desk 51
Sandy.............................123
Saracens Head, The..........110
Saxon 15
School, founding & history of 50,51,*59,60,62*
  lace 50
  Sunday 51,78

400th Anniversary of 52	Toddington...............19,55,109	West Street........................99
Scott, Thomas 100	Tollhouse....................103,104	Wheatsheaf, The.................110
Sheep Lane.......................104	Tong, James.......................54	White Bear, The 111
Sherborn, William 19,20	tower, of new church 34,35,*45*	White City ..(London End) ..
Shotters Cottage.................103	of old church 34,*43*,50,54,	White Hart, The 105,110
Shuttleworth College............36	77,*97*	White Horse, The 111
Shoulder of Mutton, The 111	Town Hall (Market House)	White Lion, The 111,*114*
Shyngleshurt, John................30	........48,49,*57,58*,71,109,111,	Whiteman, Arthur..............105
Skilton, Elisabeth 51	*114,*126,128,*137,154*	Whitman, David..................48
smallpox 54	trial, of Robert Hobbs,	Whitnoe Grange 17
Spavins, Frances..............74,77	last Abbot 18,19,20,21,*26*	Wiffen, Benjamin 100,101
Snetsler, organ of old church ..74	Tunstall..............................73	Elizabeth 100
Soulbury, Hugh de...............17	Turney, Mr..................*137,141*	Jeremiah 20,*27*,100,101,*101*
Souldrop 36	turnpike, Hockliffe/Newport	John............................100
Southey, Rev *40*	Pagnell 104	William IV......................*43*,48
Speedwell 127,128	Woburn/Ampthill.............104	William and Mary 53
stained glass..................*81,82*	Woburn/Hockliffe......103,104	Williams, John .ᴀ..............19,21
Stanton, William 50	Woburn/Leighton	Windmill, The...................111
Star Lodge 15	Buzzard 104	window, east.......................*43*
Staunton, Edward........21,29,53	Tuscan plait 51	experimental....................*83*
family 54		Woburn, Abbey of St Mary ..16,
family memorial *41*	Union Workhouse ..55,*65,67,*127	18,21,*24*,29,*89*
Francis...30,31,37,*41,43*,54,*63*	Utcoate Grange 17,21,*23*	abbot of..........16,17,22,29,30
Robert 21,29		birdcatcher *119,*126,*139*
Staveley...........................30	vestry........................35,71,92	Company of bellringers 77,
Staunton House...................*63*	Vestry Minutes 36,72	78,*95*
Steppingley....................36,54	Viatores.............................15	derivation of name 15
Stolt, William 21	Vicarage *97*	Gas Company..........56,*67,68*
Sycamore Cottage *138*	Victoria, Queen...................48	Holiday.........................110
Sykes, Mr & Mrs..................78	*Virgin and Child,* Carlo Maratti	Sheepshearing 123
	.......................34,*42,43,*73	Union 55
Tanqueray, family 74	Voelcker, Augustus..............124	Wild Life Kingdom........1215
Tavistock, Marchioness of......22	Vulliamy, Benjamin Louis .*43,*35	Woburn Sands,........29,36,100,
Marquess of 22,48,*62*	watchhouse.........................48	101,105,111,113,126,128
Three Pots, The..................110	watchman 48	Woodward, Mr D.O. 73
Thort... ...ᴿ... 53	water supply 56	Woolsack, The...................110
Tickford Bridge...................104	Watling Street..........15,103,104	Working Men's Club............78
Tilsworth 55	Wavendon 100	Wrestlers, The....................110
timber yard 127,*148*	Wenham, Rev T 74,109	Wulfstan, Saint 17
Timms, Bill *147*	Wesley, John 99	Wylwarde, John 19
Tingrith.............................55		

ENDPAPERS: Pen and ink drawings by John Rowland showing the facades of Woburn's buildings in 1974. (JR)

176

High Street

Market Place

Park Street

ge Street